Money Too for Women

Simple Solutions
for
Mastering
Your Money

by
Audrey Reed, D.S.S.
The Money Doctor

Money ToolBox™ *for Women*
Simple Solutions for Mastering Your Money

ISBN 0-9718615-0-1
Library of Congress Catalog Card Number TXU1-009-511
Published by
Works in Progress, Inc. 2002
P.O. Box 247 Minden, Nevada 89403
775-782 4639 or 888-853-6564
e-mail–info@moneytoolboxforwomen.com
www.moneytoolboxforwomen.com

Audrey Reed, D.S.S., The Money Doctor, knows

The Deep, Dark Secret of Mastering Money. . .

. . .And she reveals it in *The Money ToolBox* for Women.

But just knowing the secret isn't enough. That's where the real magic of this book comes into play. Dr. Reed pierces to the essence of working with money. This book talks to women—or anyone who's interested in gaining control over their money and enjoying prosperity—in friendly, arm-in-arm, let's-have-a-latte language. She calls them like she sees them, and presents great pictures of how certain behaviors (I still have checks, I must have money) don't work. Then she describes how to do simple, often really fun things, to transform them into behaviors that do work, and work very well.

Every section presents a tool or two you can use. And every one ends with a reminder to celebrate your successes. Along the way you get stories about people. These stories share what was learned and how these people enjoy new levels of money success.

This book is an easy read. It is filled with encouragement. It is the kind of book that has you nodding "Yes" every few sentences, knowing you can—and will—do what it recommends.

You can almost feel your life changing for the better with every page as you get deeper into the secret of making money your ally. Here is a book worth reading. . .and a secret worth knowing.

ABOUT THE AUTHOR

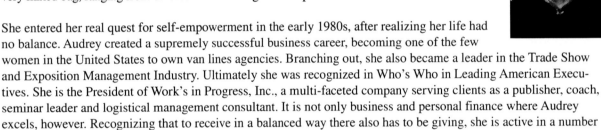

Audrey Reed, Doctor of Spiritual Science, The Money Doctor, has built her reputation for effectiveness and success in business and as an educator the old-fashioned way: She worked hard, paid attention, and learned from everything that came her way. And what came her way was a very mixed bag, ranging from divorce to swimming with dolphins.

She entered her real quest for self-empowerment in the early 1980s, after realizing her life had no balance. Audrey created a supremely successful business career, becoming one of the few women in the United States to own van lines agencies. Branching out, she also became a leader in the Trade Show and Exposition Management Industry. Ultimately she was recognized in Who's Who in Leading American Executives. She is the President of Work's in Progress, Inc., a multi-faceted company serving clients as a publisher, coach, seminar leader and logistical management consultant. It is not only business and personal finance where Audrey excels, however. Recognizing that to receive in a balanced way there also has to be giving, she is active in a number of philanthropic endeavors, acting as an advocate for women, children and the planet.

Dr. Reed holds a D.S.S. (Doctor of Spiritual Science) from Peace Theological Seminary and College of Philosophy in Los Angeles, B.A. in Business Management, certification as a Master Hypnotist and Master Trainer in NeuroLinguisticProgramming (NLP) and a three-year study degree in Ontological Design.

Among her avocations are extensive study in Native American Culture and Ritual, and she is an avid golfer and skier. Audrey remarried in 2001 and is an all-around happy camper.

Audrey Reed, D.S.S., is a speaker, seminar leader and personal/business coach.

ABOUT THE AUTHOR

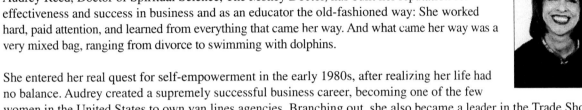

Audrey Reed, Doctor of Spiritual Science, The Money Doctor, has built her reputation for effectiveness and success in business and as an educator the old-fashioned way: She worked hard, paid attention, and learned from everything that came her way. And what came her way was a very mixed bag, ranging from divorce to swimming with dolphins.

She entered her real quest for self-empowerment in the early 1980s, after realizing her life had no balance. Audrey created a supremely successful business career, becoming one of the few women in the United States to own van lines agencies. Branching out, she also became a leader in the Trade Show and Exposition Management Industry. Ultimately she was recognized in Who's Who in Leading American Executives. She is the President of Work's in Progress, Inc., a multi-faceted company serving clients as a publisher, coach, seminar leader and logistical management consultant. It is not only business and personal finance where Audrey excels, however. Recognizing that to receive in a balanced way there also has to be giving, she is active in a number of philanthropic endeavors, acting as an advocate for women, children and the planet.

Dr. Reed holds a D.S.S. (Doctor of Spiritual Science) from Peace Theological Seminary and College of Philosophy in Los Angeles, B.A. in Business Management, certification as a Master Hypnotist and Master Trainer in NeuroLinguisticProgramming (NLP) and a three-year study degree in Ontological Design.

Among her avocations are extensive study in Native American Culture and Ritual, and she is an avid golfer and skier. Audrey remarried in 2001 and is an all-around happy camper.

Audrey Reed, D.S.S., is a speaker, seminar leader and personal/business coach.

Audrey Reed, D.S.S., The Money Doctor, knows

The Deep, Dark Secret of Mastering Money. . .

. . .And she reveals it in *The Money ToolBox* for Women.

But just knowing the secret isn't enough. That's where the real magic of this book comes into play. Dr. Reed pierces to the essence of working with money. This book talks to women—or anyone who's interested in gaining control over their money and enjoying prosperity—in friendly, arm-in-arm, let's-have-a-latte language. She calls them like she sees them, and presents great pictures of how certain behaviors (I still have checks, I must have money) don't work. Then she describes how to do simple, often really fun things, to transform them into behaviors that do work, and work very well.

Every section presents a tool or two you can use. And every one ends with a reminder to celebrate your successes. Along the way you get stories about people. These stories share what was learned and how these people enjoy new levels of money success.

This book is an easy read. It is filled with encouragement. It is the kind of book that has you nodding "Yes" every few sentences, knowing you can—and will—do what it recommends.

You can almost feel your life changing for the better with every page as you get deeper into the secret of making money your ally. Here is a book worth reading. . .and a secret worth knowing.

Dedication

This book is dedicated to my daughter,
Kimberly Anne Reed.
It is an honoring of who she is becoming.

Dr. Reed, ala Mary Poppins has created "sugar" that "helps the medicine go down," taking a potentially difficult subject and making it palatable and fun while giving useful tips and ways to develop lifelong changes in behavior..

—Lynne Tracy, M.A.

"I hope mothers of all ages read this book immediately for their daughters' sake. Then pass it on. Thanks for addressing this critical issue."

—Renee Singer Goldberg
Co-President, Eastboard Consoles Inc.
Philadelphia, PA

A wise and simple book on how women relate to money and abundance, *Money ToolBox for Women*, is a "must read" for women on the path to money mastery!

—Linda Nobel Topf, Author,
You Are Not Your Illness:
Seven principles for Meeting the Challenge.
iCan! Columnist and Spiritual Advisor.

Table of Contents

Table of Contents continued

Table of Contents continued

Foreword

This book is about MONEY. Any Money—Little or Big.

It's also about creating abundance in your life. It has smiles.

It is a place for creating new practices. That's rigor.

Historically, money has seemed complex. These Tools are simple.

Think of this book as a magical toolbox filled with precious golden tools. Use the Tools to build successes in your money life. Share your wisdom.

The Tools can shift your money views. That's luscious!

The Tools are developed so you can use them every day. They are Gracefully basic.

The Tools are easy to practice. No School Karma!

In this book there are stories, examples, metaphors and places to write and draw. It's delightful.

As you enjoy this book you will discover—YOU ARE NOT ALONE!

Journey with your fellow travelers to a place of competence and new strategies with money.

ARE YOU READY?   Let's Begin!

Introduction

<u>You are not Alone</u>

This book is for all women. It is especially for women who believe they are alone in the world of MONEY.

Do you wonder where your money goes?

Is your belief that you could never learn to take care of your MONEY?

Do you believe you are not smart about MONEY, no matter what your educational level?

When you start to think about MONEY, do you take "the head in the sand" approach? (I used to do that.)

Do you have the MONEY basics, MONEY tools? Do you apply them?

What I discovered is that when it comes to money, many women are carrying it around in a bucket with a hole in it. It is the hole of unawareness or even willful ignorance. What I also discovered, and am still discovering, is *how to mend the hole in the bucket*.

We have the ability to nurture our money, abundance, prosperity, riches and our selves.
Many of us do not do it. *You are not alone.*

The ToolBox

Imagine that this book is a toolbox filled with simple practices to guide you into **money honoring** and abundance. It is a workbook—or, better yet, a play book. It has stories , mostly composite learnings from fabulous women's sharings; these are **tool stories**. It has processes. It has practices that are designed to develop strong skills.

Each area is designed and written from a heart space of loving and growth, gratitude and devotion. The practices *will* make money work. Use what works for you.

Together, let's journey into developing skills around money.
It will shift your life. You will love it!

<u>Why the journey?</u>

This book was written thanks to my daughter, Kimberly. The tools we discovered in our journey together have made her a woman who is more respecting, effective and efficient with money. She has allowed her story to be told throughout this book.

Kimberly reflects that the process of making money a friend, while usually simple, is not always easy. There is a certain addiction to spending—it is truly a drugged state of mind.

Kimberly never realized how much money she was spending. She is brilliant in most domains, but in the domain of money, she did not have the tools to figure it out alone.

It didn't matter how much she read; old habits were more practiced than the new possibilities. It was almost always one step forward, two steps back.

She, as others we have talked with, reported that the books about finance were too complex. They were difficult to consume and voluminous. They put us on information overload. Kimberly said she lost focus between the words of the language of finance. Even when she did understand some of it, she wondered how to apply the practices in her life because they were so complex. Here, the tools are simple.

Kimberly now has a different awareness of this syndrome which keeps her awake to the monsters of her own behaviors. She is honoring herself and honoring the flow of her own money. She is actually out of credit card debt and saving for her future. There's much more!

If There's One, There are Others.

If there is one woman experiencing this, there are other women. Are you one of them? Together Kimberly, myself and a group of women friends began to discuss how we handled our money. It opened up very intimate, old, and hidden conversations surrounding money we had stored inside of us. We found we were holding these as "pictures" in our minds and they were influencing our current choices and behaviors. We have used these conversations in **Tool #2: <u>Snapshots.</u>** In our process, we traded our old stories in for the learnings and blessing each could become. Now we are easily applying the learnings and enjoying the blessings.

How Did We Get Here?

Getting to this point took a while. It involved a bunch of things: Research. Reading. Questioning women. And men.
Finding out what works? What doesn't?

We asked things like: How did you learn? When did you know to stop doing something that was supposed to be working and wasn't? Can the subject of money be filled with humor, Light and spiritual loving?

As a community of women, we began to realize there are choices in relationship to our MONEY. Practices and tools began to come together.

There was Light!

We sought actions that would shake the piggy banks of our lives. What actions were practical? Which tools were simple and effective? What actions would change the way we respect and honor money? What behavioral shifting would change negative **money talk?** How would these changes shape our relationship to money and our view of abundance?

In the end, we came to the conclusion that money wasn't, of itself, secret or mysterious, or even really difficult to love and nurture. We just needed to rearrange the way we looked at it, thought about it, listened to it, related to it, played with it and embraced it. And we discovered there were ways—most of them even fun and easy—to do that.

Here they are. We did this for us. We share it with you.

A Word About Tools

Tools, by definition, will work to make your life easier. There's just one catch: You have to use the tool. Just owning the tool, sharpening the tool, putting the tool in a nice display box, talking about the tool, showing the tool to your friends, and admiring the tool will not do anything. It's not until you scrape the peeler across the carrot, or hammer the nail into the board that you get the value of simple tools.

All these tools work. We know, because we worked them. They may not all work for you all the time. That's fine.

Your challenge is to try each tool and see what it does. If things get better, keep using the tool. If nothing changes, go on to another tool. Revisit the tools that you set aside, from time to time. As you gain skill with one tool, you might find you have gained a new skill with another tool.

Have a great time. Enjoy the new skills and learnings. Be uplifted by the stories of other women and play with the tools in a way that works for you.

Tool #1
Money Writing:

We know, everyone from Oprah to you-name-it talks about the benefits of keeping a journal. That's just the point: There must be value to it if so many people are endorsing it. Count us among those who find value in writing about our concerns, issues and gratitudes around money

The journal we are presenting as a tool is a little different. It's about (what else?) money, and you can simply write a sentence or two a day.
Writing is a way for you to step outside of yourself and have a conversation with yourself.

The practice of writing gives you the tool of observation. Choosing to use this tool, you will see that **money writing** each day changes your perspective on your money concerns and issues. Believe us: It is good for your soul.

Getting lighter—when you write there is a release. You drop some of the rocks (historical beliefs) that have been weighing you down. Lifting your spirit, you gain vision.

Here are some questions to guide you: What have been your money problems?
What are your current concerns about money?
What have been your solutions?

What future vision can you imagine for yourself, that you can step into?
What abundances are present for you today?
What are you grateful for today?

The writing tool takes practice. It can take sixty seconds or a half-hour. You will see how useful it becomes as we venture into your **money life photo album** in Tool #2, Snapshots.

Have a great time.   Make it fun $$$$$.
Simple Wisdom: Writing gives you altitude—an angel's eye view to receive new instructions. You will gain broader vision from higher altitude.
Altitude reveals your abundance.
Recognizing Abundance brings you gratitude.
Gratitude gives you focus.
Focus provides the ability to manifest.
Manifestation completes the circle of money.

Now You are ready for the TOOL, _Snapshots._

Tool # 2
<u>Snapshots:</u>

Inner money talk creates pictures in your mind.

Changing the talk changes the inner money pictures and that automatically changes your **money life**.

When it comes to money, many of us (okay, most of us—even people who have a lot of money) are lugging around a sack of rocks: old beliefs and programmings that affect our behavior and our attitudes about money. Get rid of the sack of rocks you are carrying.

<u>Snapshots</u> is a process of looking at simple money moments in your money life, frozen in time. These old <u>snapshots</u> are some of the reasons for the way you are

with your money. They are the rocks.

Old <u>snapshots</u> can keep you stuck in old behaviors. Here is the TOOL to catapult you into new, joyful behavior around money.   You can use this tool now or when your rocks (money concerns or issues) appear. It will come in handy, everywhere and anywhere.

It is about change.

Tool Story

This is the detail of my own story. My heart still fills with gratitude when I think of how the **Snapshots** Tool changed my life.

Old snapshot:
I was 42, working 60 hours a week in my entrepreneurial business, recently

divorced and tired. My daughter was grown; sometimes home, sometimes not.

During the marriage, my husband had paid the mortgage, all necessary expenses and vacations. I had spent most of my money on keeping up with *our* lifestyle and my daughter's education. I observed this snapshot from the place of ***"This will never end."***

Now it was over. I was afraid. "How would I do this?" My voice was that of a 4-year old.

Who I was just before using the snapshot methodology:
I am 52 years old. I survived. The fear still comes and goes in my chest. The fear is from ten years ago. I still carry it with me on some days.
After the snapshot methodology process I wrote:

How would I handle the picture today?

I would hear myself saying to myself, "I will survive. I am resilient. I have the ability to take care of myself and my daughter." I would be talking to my girl-friends. I would be talking about the fears. I would work it out with professionals. I would shine the loving flashlight on my fears; recognize I was not alone. I would disappear the fears one at a time. I would see myself hugging myself. I would see myself focused forward. I would keep sharing my feelings and releasing the fear of the unknown and the remorse.

Old Snapshot to New Picture:

New snapshot: I am 42 years old, sitting on my bed talking to my friends and we are strategizing about our futures. I am focused and joy-filled. I am learning about respecting and spending money wisely. I am feeling comfortable with my decisions.

SNAP!

Result:
The rock I have been dragging around disappears!

Money Lesson:
All things change. Save and invest for the future.

Money Blessing:
I have learned to be resilient. I have learned about money, spending, and saving.
I am abundant. I am grateful for my life day by day.

When I tested out this tool for the first time I was amazed. I had been carrying around intermittent fear for about ten years, ever since my divorce. I realized that this fear was based on a picture I had created with my fearful self-talk. I applied the snapshot tool and the fear virtually dissolved. I easily and very naturally slipped into the confident, happy person in the new picture.

SNAPSHOT METHODOLOGY

Journal the event you intend to change. (You only need a sentence or two about the *money moment.*)

- Take whatever you need to be comfortable; a blanket, some pillows, a glass of water. You will also take a very special new tool, an imaginary LOVING FLASHLIGHT.
- Find a comfortable spot. (Sometimes I go to the bathroom and make a blanket and pillow nest in the tub.)

Starting point: Relax! We use this tool all the time to just get balanced in those what-did-I do-that-for moments…read through it once, you will find the process begins automatically. Then read it again and again as issues come forward during the rest of the book.

- Imagine you are a photographer setting up a scene in the photo album of your life. As the photographer, you can make any adjustments you choose.   Your wonderful inventive camera has a volume control you can adjust to make sure everything is sounds just the way you want it.

- Turn on the camera. Test the adjustments & sound.
- See/hear the money moment (snapshot).
- See/hear yourself at the age of the snapshot. Remind yourself that you are the age you are now (_____) and in your comfortable and safe place.
- You may have some emotions. Observe if the emotions are from the past or they originate now. Take a moment to breathe.
- Take out your LOVING FLASHLIGHT and shine it on the snapshot. As you bring in the Brightness. it will begin to release what bothers you about the moment.

- Now ask yourself some questions:
  How would I handle the same situation now?
  What different choices would I make today?

- As you see or hear the answers to your question, change the images or sounds in your snapshot. See yourself as your wiser and more, experienced self, in the picture. Use the years of wisdom you have gained since the picture was formed.
- Turn the LOVING FLASHLIGHT on the picture again. Shine that love on the people in the picture or conversation.
- Replace the old _snapshot_ by watching the people change.
- Observe how the picture shifts. Hear the new words. You are the wise one. See yourself change in the snapshot. How does that feel?
- As the new picture comes into clearer focus, ask yourself:
- What is the **money lesson**? Write it down if you want to.

- What is the **money blessing**? Write it down if you want to.
- As you hear or see or feel these answers, breathe them in.

- Shine your flashlight on the scene until the new picture or conversation is fully developed. Keep it shining until your heart is filled with Light.
- See/hear the blessing, clearly.
- Snap the fully developed moment, now.
- Turn off the camera

- Take a few minutes to place this new picture in your new **money life photo album**.
- Write in your journal using the checklist on the next page.
- Get a drink of water.
- Take some time to be comfortable with the new learnings and blessing.

CHECKLIST

As you settle in with your new picture, check off the following points and adjust anything that may need it.

1. Old snapshot is changed.
2. New picture in place.
3. Grateful for the lesson.
4. Celebrate the Blessing.
5. Breathe into the newness of the experience.
6. Use this TOOL as often as you like. Even for current <u>snapshots.</u>
7. Write Here!

Write Here

Stars _____ here.

Celebrate!

Tools #3 & #4
<u>BIG MAMA's Pocketbook</u>

We are going to dive right into the center of our hearts and pocketbooks. My Mama told me that my pocketbook was the soul of "a girl's walking around equipment," pocketbooks are where our money lives.

Tool #3 and #4 are about respecting and honoring money.

Simple Wisdom: Keep your money organized.

Every woman has a pocketbook, briefcase, knapsack or bag. I've been inside some of these bags. Each one I've seen is in some state of chaos: combs, brushes, makeup, day books, palm pilots, cell phones, money in a zipper compartment, money just thrown in after a hurried purchase, and change everywhere.

Tool Story:

My friend Rachel and I are standing in line at a coffee place near my house in Santa Monica, CA. She's frantically digging in her knapsack. She has zipped and unzipped each pocket and rummaged in each one at least twice. All through the process she is muttering to herself, "Where is it?" over and over again. Finally, I cannot stand it. "What are you searching for?"

"I just had it," she snaps.

"What?" I ask in as comforting a voice as I can muster.

"My $10 bill. It was right here this morning—now it's gone. I don't know where I put it, and now I can't pay for our coffee."

We dumped the knapsack on the table and searched: make-up, gum, crumpled up paper, notebook, pens, hair gel, wallet (no money), old business cards, on and on and on. Suddenly she looked up and, with a grin of embarrassment, she reached into her jeans pocket and produced the money. "I had it in a place where I could get to it fast in line," Rachel smiled sheepishly. We both laughed at a good plan gone bad and at the contents of the knapsack on the table.

Keep it together!
Keep it straight!
Keep it orderly!
HOW? HOW? HOW? Keep reading.

MONEY TOOLBOX FOR WOMEN

Mini - Tool

Here's a great way to handle change build-up. Keep a few quarters, 2 dimes, 2 nickels, and 4 pennies in your wallet or coin carrier. For the rest of your loose change, create a change box in a drawer, and every night put your extra change there. Guess what: By the end of the month, you'll have about $30.00 - $ 45.00 of "found money."

My sister-in-law used the mini tool of saving her change each day. She ended up with enough money to buy most of her Christmas presents one year. Amazing!

We've heard the old adage " **Time is Money**." However, money requires time to be cared for, counted, cultivated, and created. Also, there is an elegance in learning gradually, so you can get it into your bones, create new habits and new behaviors. This is one of those tiny steps you can take to produce big results. Relax. Breathe. Focus Forward.

Tool #3 begins with keeping your money in order. Order shows honor and respect. The line of energy that money is can grow and multiply in the energy field of orderliness.

Tool #3
Mini Cash Drawer

Arrange a special place that is clean and clear of anything else.

Go now to the pocketbook, knapsack, briefcase or carrybag that you use every day.

Dump it!

Amidst all the inevitable clutter, what does the money look like inside? How much was there in all the different places and spaces?
Watch out for the GIANT FROG that got caught in the bottom of your bag!

Take out your money from all the places and spaces in your purse. Take out all the money in your wallet, your pocketbook, and from your pockets or any place else you may be hiding it. Now get ready to organize it. Right, organize it.

Banks and stores keep the money in cash drawers for order. People, especially women, often don't. You get money back and what you do with it has no rhyme or reason.

What do you do? Most likely, toss it in your purse. Thus the small mountain in front of you. That's sloppy. There's no rigor. No flow. No orderliness.

Give your money rigor and order. See if it doesn't make a difference in your abundance.

(We'll find even more money with the ***Tool, Cracks and Crevices***. Now, our focus is on the money stash in your carrying-around equipment.)

Start by uncrumpling the bills you've retrieved from the bottom of your carry bag.

Unfold the bills that were hidden away.

Feel the money.

Make a neat pile for each denomination.

| $ 1 | $5 | $10 | $20 | $50 | $100 |

Money likes orderliness.

And money thrives when it is part of a collective. The energy of money knows how much it is as a community of funds available.

Face all the money in the same direction: Faces all facing up, bills arranged the same way.

Admire the neatness of it all.

Now, find a place in your wallet or purse where you will keep your money. All your money. All the time. Put your money in there.

Take it out, look at it, then put it back in the same place.

Do this a couple of times so you will get used to how it feels to do it. And do it each time you change purses or knapsacks, so you know exactly where your money will be when you want it.

Just wait until you need to find your $10 bill to pay for your next _____.
You will be thrilled to find it every time right in the place it's supposed to be.

Point of Awareness: 8 out of 10 wealthy people, keep money in order.
Nurture - Respect
Honor - Attract

Star____Here.

Celebrate!

Tool #4
<u>The Queen Was In The Counting House...</u>

Each morning, count the money in your purse. Know how much you are starting out with today and every day from now on.

At the end of the spending day, recount the money. This way you know how much you've spent during the day. You'll also know how much you have for tomorrow. (More about this Tool <u>In Daily Expenses</u>.)

This is not about being a miser and counting your money to hoard it. This is about letting the energy flow of money find itself, and bringing money to money.

(If you have a secret money $$$$ place, that's fine. However, keep it consistent, i.e., stash your hidden money in a place where you can keep track of it. And, count it daily with the rest of your money $$$$.)

You know, the rich get richer and that's no accident. There is a focus and attention. It brings forward the line of energy.

Money Attracts Money
Like Attracts Like
It's Physics - It's Life

Celebrate what you've done. Celebration is whatever makes you feel good. At the end of each chapter there is always a time to celebrate yourself. Below are some ideas. Add your own celebration ideas to the page. Celebrate yourself often.
Star ____Here.
It will nurture you into abundance.

Celebration ideas:

Take a walk.

Hug a Tree

Sit in the Sun

Spend the rest of your day in your pajamas (this is a real treat for me)

Stand up and jump around. Get moving!

Turn on some music and sing.

Have a run with the dog.

Pet the cat.

Get dressed up.

Have some tea.

Light candles.

Hug your spouse, lover, friend.

Take a bubble bath.

Go Play

Go to the movies.

Enjoy the flowers
Go to the local park and swing or just watch the kids play.
Move your body.
Relax.
Take a five minute mini-vacation in your imagination.
Take time for you in a special and good way, even if it's only 15 minutes.
Do things with friends that you can share together: manicures, pedicures, massage each other's hands, comb each other's hair
Have a glass of _____ together in celebration.
Sit in a garden.
Go to the Zoo
Nap
Read your favorite children's book

Nurture yourself abundant!
Write a thank you note to yourself.

What is it you love to do? Write it here:

Do it now.
CELEBRATE a new awareness, a new practice and a shiny new tool.
Give yourself another star ___ here.

Tool #5
Cracks and Crevices – Where Money Hides

This Tool is about finding money. It is a process of choosing to rediscover the spaces and places where money is left, often forgotten and abandoned. You will discover money hidden in some strange places. This is your personal invitation to uncover all the places money is lost or left and reclaim it so you can enjoy it.

Start with this prayer. (Really, say it.)
A prayer for St. Anthony, the Saint who finds lost items:
St. Anthony, St. Anthony
Please return _____ to me.
(Repeat 4 X.)

You'll be amazed. Use it. The prayer works.

Take the time to do this activity. You will be surprised. Maybe you won't find hundreds of dollars…however you could find enough to take yourself and a friend out to celebrate with your newfound abundance.

Do this practice with a friend. You go to her house, then she can come over to yours. Share the wealth. Be open to community. Make it a party!

Example
I called Kimberly and asked her to try out this Tool. She reported she'd just completed this task and knew where every penny was found. She insisted there was no more hidden money. My response was, "That's what you think! If it worked once, it will work again."

When I arrived at Kimberly's I was greeted by her challenging smirk. "I looked *everywhere*, so you're wasting your time.

I shrugged "Maybe, but what a great excuse to hang out together. I imagine you looked under the pillows in the couch."

"Of course." Kimberly rolled her eyes. "And in all my old purses. I'm telling you I looked everywhere."

"You know, I found a ten dollar bill behind my dresser where it must have fallen when I was switching purses."

Kimberly's smirk started to slip.

"And darned if I didn't find a couple dollars in change in my bathroom drawers. I haven't the foggiest idea how it got there."

By the end of the time we spent looking together we found another seven or eight dollars, and Kimberly and I were toasting this tool with a glass of sparkling water.

What works, works. This Tool works every time. It is an adventure into our daily habits. It is a time to look at the places and spaces where money hides, is misplaced, or goes to the land of the lost or missing. (Unlike socks that disappear in the dryer and turn into all those extra hangers in the closet, money doesn't go anywhere. It just sits there waiting to be found. By making an effort to find it at one time, you don't just end up with a quarter here and a dime there. You end up with real money that you can use or have fun with. It's found wealth!)

Every once in a while, someone tells me they have no hidden money. Don't believe it. Everyone has it. But it's hidden, that's why they don't know they have it.

Tool #5
It's a scavenger hunt.

Below is a list of places you can look for hidden money. Look in all the places on the list. Then look wherever else you think you have left or lost forgotten treasures. You could remember where the bonus money is buried. Even if you don't, look in all these places, and then look in others you discover along the way.

Knapsacks
Desk drawers
Brief cases
Kitchen drawers & cabinets
Bureaus
Ash trays
Glasses in bathrooms
Laundry room shelf

Golf club bag
Tennis bag
Bowling bag
Any other bag
Airplane carry-on
Small box on bookshelf

Name the other places forgotten or where you did not know to look.
Write them here.

_____

_____

_____

_____

_____

_____

_____

Keep looking until you feel complete.

I'm continually amazed at the success stories about this tool. I'll share some with you.

Tool Story #1

My roommate, Jona, and I began the research to see if this theory had substance. We challenged one another: Who could find the most hidden $$$ during the first hunt? We were ruthless as we scavenged through pockets and coats, gym bags, old pocketbooks, books. (Yes, books. I sometimes take a $10.00 bill out of my wallet and go to get coffee and a snack with just a book and my glasses. I'll put the change in my pocket, but the bills I'll use as a bookmarker. Guess what? Sometimes the money is still marking a spot years later.)
We did this exercise twice. The first time we found $170.00. The second time, we discovered another $80.00. This does not count the refundable airline ticket in the

inside pocket of my winter coat that was returned by the company that stores and cleans the coats. It was good for $297.00. Thank you, Linda Berkowitz, Miller and Berkowitz, New York City.

Girlfriend Confessions

One girlfriend keeps money in a box in her desk, and that's okay. But she throws any foreign currency she has left over from trips in this box and never converts the money to U.S. dollars. At my suggestion she finally cashed it in. Total $123.00.

Another woman keeps $100 cash in her car for emergencies and we found an additional $289 in other drawers, pockets, desk, pocketbooks and brief cases. Total $389.

One of my friends keeps change in a drinking cup in her kitchen cabinet, a jar on her dresser and dollars, safely hidden, between two pictures in a photo album. Total $87.00.

Found $175.00 total as we sorted through a friend's things, getting ready for a garage sale.

Found $300.00 in the place where someone normally keeps $100.00 for salon services. Talk about money growing.

Girls aren't the only ones who do this.
Denny wondered why his briefcase had become so heavy over the last few days…accumulated amount of change: $11.00.

Again, do it with a friend or friends…it's more fun, and it takes the work out of the process. Put on your favorite dance music to create a high-energy day.

Where did your money hide? Help us add to our list. (www.moneytoolboxforwomen.com) Email (info@moneytoolboxfor women.com) or mail your surprise places to us so we can add them to our list and assist others.

I clean my money hiding places once a year! Sure enough, as soon as I think I've got this handled it happens again: More money in strange places.

Point of awareness: One of my favorite finance teachers always walks looking down at the street. He's found lots of money on the ground by being present with what was around him that had been unconsciously abandoned by others.

One last tool story.

My associate, Lorraine, found 2 camera lenses she'd forgotten to return. A year had passed. The lenses were hidden (undoubtedly by **Closet Trolls**) on a shelf in her closet, still in the box with all the paper work. She called the company. They took back the lenses and credited her credit card. Payoff: a couple hundred extra dollars.

Found $$$$. It's everywhere!
Star_____Here
Celebrate!

Tool #6
Where do you spend your money?

Abundance Is a Process of Consciousness.

Tool #6 is about becoming an observer of where you think you spend your money.

Some financial books might label this practice "creating a budget." It is not! Budgets are future-based possibilities of income and expenses based on past information, formulated for the present.

Do we really know how much we spend on items, other than those which are guaranteed the same month after month? There is no guarantee how much your electric bill will be next month or what gas or grocery prices will be tomorrow. The new question to filter your expenses through is, "How do you **now** spend your money?"

This question will allow you to view how much money you believe you spend. **Tool #8**, <u>**In Daily Expenses**</u>, tracks what you really spend.

Knowledge is freedom. Applying this tool is a way to set yourself free.

Just so you know, some people tend to skim over this Tool. It can be uncomfortable. Uncomfortable is normal with growth.

Also for your awareness, people generally find they are spending about twenty-five percent—yes, 25%—more than they think they are spending.

If you don't know how much you spend, how will you know how much you need to be earning? As you begin this practice, remember, knowledge will set you free— money freedom is just around the corner.

My daughter Kimberly did this process and realized how much she would have to earn, net, (after taxes and benefits) to continue her lifestyle. It was a shock. She asked herself two questions in order to create a new vision for her **money life**: (1) what did she really want in her life and (2) what was she currently spending her money for that she really didn't want, need or desire. The answers to these questions were not about lack or deprivation. They were about choice.

The knowledge you gain from using **Tool #6**, and from the following three tools, will let you know what you need to earn if you want to continue your current lifestyle spending. These tools help create a place from which to ask questions. Why do I spend my money on this or that? Do I really want to spend my money on this? Think about the empowerment and freedom you can have from really knowing these things.

This Tool is designed to naturally change your behaviors. It is formulated to bring you into alignment with your money and abundance.
It is a creative process.

Tool #6 is a first step. It assists you in investigating where you *think* you spend your money.

Later, in **Tool #8**, you will consider tracking how you spend your money. However, this practice begins the process of heightening your awareness. It develops a rigor in your conscious thinking of how your money is used on the planet. If you are like many of us who have done these particular processes, you will find some very interesting surprises.

TOOL #6

Where do you think you spend your money?

Be expansive in this process. Know this: There are no wrong answers. There's No School Karma! You will have many opportunities to check, evaluate and rethink your present spending habits. They are neither good nor bad. Right now you just want to find out what they are.

So just begin. If you are in a relationship and share financial responsibilities, I recommend you do this with your partner. If your partner doesn't want to play, do it yourself. Your new questions and attention to how you are spending your money will almost certainly call them to the game.

These are luscious learnings. Declare yourself abundant. Choose Joy!

Here is a list to help you get started considering where your money goes. This list is not complete, so please add other categories. Look through your checkbook to see other places your money goes. Your credit card statement will also provide clues.

Have fun with this. It is a tool for gaining awareness, and awareness is power!

	$$$$ Amount You think you spend	Real $$$$ Actually spend
Rent or Mortgage		
Groceries:		
Supermarket		
Health food store		
(can include supplements)		
Farmer's market		
Other specialty food stores		
Supplements:		
Vitamins		
Minerals		
Homeopathics		
Others		

Clothes:
    Work
    Play
Others (I have a separate section for stockings)
Utilities:
    Gas (house)
    Electric
    Sewer
    Water
    Bottled Water
    Trash Collection
Taxes:
    Real estate
    State
    Local

$$$$ Amount You think you spend	Real $$$$ Actually spend

	$$$$ Amount You think you spend	Real $$$$ Actually spend
IRA		
Automobile:		
Gas		
Repairs		
Tags		
Parking		
Insurance:		
Car		
House		
Rental		
Health Care		
Dental		
Prescriptions		
Life		

	$$$$ Amount You think you spend	Real $$$$ Actually spend
Beauty Products		
Personal Care Services		
Hair Cuts		
Manicures		
Pedicures		
Hair Coloring		
Massage		
Entertainment:		
Eating out		
Breakfasts		
Lunches		
Dinners		
Coffee		
Movies		

	$$$$ Amount You think you spend	Real $$$$ Actually spend
Theater		
Clubs		
Music/Concerts		
Sports Activities:		
Golf		
Skiing		
Bike Accessories		
Gifts (self and others)		
Books		
Cable TV		
Internet Services		
Alcoholic Beverages		
Home		
Smoking		

	$$$$ Amount You think you spend	Real $$$$ Actually spend

Photos/ film and developing
Dry Cleaning
Pets
Financial/Investing Services
Banking Services
Vacation
Savings
Be sure to add all the other categories
and places where you spend money.

_____

_____

_____

_____

_____

	$$$$ Amount You think you spend	Real $$$$ Actually spend

_____

_____

_____

_____

What ELSE? Where ELSE? How ELSE do you spend your money?

After you list them add the dollar amounts of all your expenses together to see how much you think you spend and what you spend it on.

(Fill this in after tool #7-8)

Total Expenses   _____   Real Expenses_____

Where you think you spend your money.   Reality!

Now, take a break. Do something nurturing for yourself. Yes, we are glad this part is over. Relax and take a breather.
Star _____ (make that two stars) HERE!

There is more to do with the list after you have completed Tool #7 and Tool #8. These processes will complete your exploration into **Where you spend your money**.

Come back to this list after **Tool #7**, **Creepy Crawlers**, and **Tool #8**, **In Daily Expenses**.

Stay with me here! Love yourself for who you are and acknowledge yourself for what a great job you've done to be here on this planet. This lesson is a gift that has been given to you. Use it completely.

Tool #7
<u>Creepy Crawlers</u>

A few months after we began to research the practices for the **Money ToolBox**, I got a call from Kimberly …she was laughing and whooping…jubilantly— in between the laughter exclaiming, "I have a flat tire."

"And you are happy?" I am confused.

I could practically see her head nodding up and down as Kimberly continued, "Yes, and I have the money in my **angel envelope** for repairs to pay for two new tires, so the front end stays balanced. Mom, it's working. A year ago this incident would have been a **creepy crawler**…thanks."

Tool #7 is about **Creepy Crawlers**; those expenses that we don't think about until they show up and crawl all over you. This is the spending that puts us into a spin. It is that place of, "OH, WHY ME GOD?" or "OH NO, I FORGOT ALL ABOUT THIS."

Tool #7 is the path to recognizing and managing **Creepy Crawlers**. Let's take a look at them. Then you can add them to the list of monthly expenses. This tool will guide you to monthly money competency.

Creepy Crawlers are actually part of the monthly expenses. They are the bills that demand large chunks of money, quarterly, semi-annually, or even annually. Because **Creepy Crawlers** are not regular, they are unexpected. Normally, we do not accumulate money for the payment of these expenses until the bill arrives.

SURPRISE!

Creepy Crawlers are the money eaters. They creep up on you and crawl all over your expectation of what expenditures you have for the month.

The side effects of **creepy crawlers**: stress, anxiety, regret, remorse, sheer terror, fight or flight, illness and "Oh my God, how am I going to pay this bill?"

Tool #7

So let's name your **creepy crawlers**. In naming things, they are not so illusive and frightening. Naming allows us to look at what needs to be done, rather than hiding our heads in the sand and hoping they will magically disappear.

We've already named some of them on the list in **Tool #6**.
At the end of this tool, we will transfer the new **creepy crawlers** to the **Where You Spend Your Money,** *WUSY$$$$,* list in the previous chapter.

List:	$$$$ Amount Here	Real $$$$ You think you spend
Car Insurance		
Car Registration Fees		
Renewal of Driver's Licenses		
Taxes		
Think of things that you might buy in bulk.		
What are the things you spend your money on only once a year?		
Shampoo you buy in bulk		
Memberships		
Birthdays		
Christmas Presents		
Doctor		

	$$$$ Amount Here	Real $$$$ You think you spend
Dentist		
Flowers		
Spring Plants (outdoors)		
Emergency Funds		
Tires		
Car Repairs		
Tune-up		
School Activities for the Kids		
School Tuition for you		

List More below:

_____

_____

_____

_____

_____

This is an awareness process. It takes you to abundance, prosperity, peace and harmony between you and your money.

Important:
Now, put your **Creepy Crawlers** on your **Where You Spend Your Money** list, in the previous chapter. Divide the $$$$ amount into <u>monthly</u> payments. Example: If you see the Dentist twice a year @ $60 a visit per person in your household, the formula would be: $60 X 2 = $120 X __ (number of people in household) = _____ Divided By 12 = $____.
That's your *Where You Spend Your Money $$$$ per month* for the Dentist.

Have fun with all this>>>>>>>>Breathe and Relax.
Celebrate Your New Knowledge!

Creepy Crawlers into

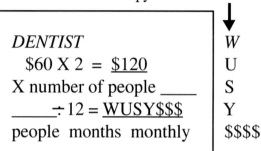

DENTIST

  $60 X 2 = <u>$120</u>

X number of people ____   S

____ ÷ 12 = <u>WUSY$$$</u>   Y

people   months   monthly $$$$

W
U

This *TOOL* is complete.

CELEBRATE YOUR LIFE!

Go take a walk, go to the movies, have a juice, or do anything you really love to do. You're doing terrific!

STARS ____ HERE.

Your Treasure Chest for In Daily Expenses and Angel Envelops

Mini-Tool

This mini-tool shows you how to set up, divide and organize your expenses into segments. It is an easy way to become rigorous with your money. You learn to save for the next month's expenses and payments.

Find a box—about X x X inches and deep enough to neatly hold business or personal size envelopes, depending on which size you choose to use for your **Angel Envelopes**, **Tool #9**. Decorate it. Make it beautiful and celebratory. (See the picture on page 73 for ideas.) It is a special symbol of your abundance and prosperity. It is a sacred offering to yourself in celebration of your present and future. (If you don't want to do the crafty part of this mini-tool, go directly to **Tool #8**.)

This is your TREASURE CHEST.
It is a place of new beginnings.
It is the place where you come for the magic to begin.
It nurtures the nature of your abundance and aligns your money.
It is the place where you begin to discover more of your abundance.
It holds awe, wonder and loving.
It holds curiosity and devotion to yourself and your family.
It holds the future of all you choose to be.
It holds golden treasure and future dreams.
It holds the blessing of practical tools for abundance and riches.

The need to be at peace with your abundance has been buried, time out of mind. This is your journey to developing a deeper relationship with your money. It is an awakening to a new abundance, joy and positive actions.

Use it with respect and honor.

Honor yourself and respect the energy and flow of the universe.

Treasure Chest

Paint it.

Use your hot glue gun to paste or stick hearts, angels, jewels, and coins—whatever symbolizes abundance and prosperity for you.

Let yourself soar.

This is a play time.

Nurture your $$$$ energy now.

Tool #8
<u>*In Daily Expenses*</u>

Tool #8 is about knowing.

Do you know how much money you need to make each month? Knowing is accomplished by research/tracking. The practice developed for **Tool #8** will strengthen your *knowing muscles*. This tool focuses on where you really spend your money. It is a 30-60 day exercise, depending on how attuned you are to how and where you spend your money.

Clarity:
If at the end of 30 days, you are still uncertain about **how and where you spend your money, continue the process for another 30 days. Compare the two months.** Compare your <u>**In Daily Expenses**</u> to the <u>**Where You Spend Your**</u>

Money list, **Tool #6**. After the next 30-60 days, you will have a good overview of how much money you will need to fulfill your financial wants, needs and desires.

At the end of 30 days

LIST	EST$	REAL$
rent		
lunch		
parking		

Fill in the
REAL$ Amounts
From In Daily Expenses

Then you'll know *Where you spend your money*, REALLY!

Tool #8 will also give you the opportunity to see where you want to spend your money and where you do not want to spend your money. **Choice**.

Money Freedom.
Choosing Yourself Abundant.

None of this is about lack or deprivation. It is about choice. Choosing feels sooo empowering. It is done from a place of loving yourself into abundance and celebration. It is the loving spirit that fills your money life with grace and ease. DO you WANT IT? COME ON - GET IT!

Tool #8

THIS IS THE CHECKLIST FOR HOW YOU REALLY SPEND YOUR MONEY.

Instructions:

In your Treasure Chest,
put a package of 4 x 6 rainbow-colored
index cards and dividers.

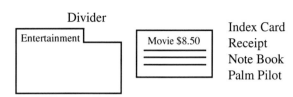

How to use them.
The **dividers** will have the same items listed as the expenses listed on the ***where you spend your money*** list. These are your **<u>In Daily Expense</u>** dividers.

The dividers go in the front of your Treasure Chest with some index cards placed behind each divider. (Divider Heading: – Entertainment. Sample Index Card headings: – Movie –Video rental – Night out dancing).

Put 5 or 6 cards in high volume purchase areas for items you might spend money on each day.

Once you have completed this you are ready for the next step: Start getting Receipts for **everything.** Put the receipts in the **<u>IN DAILY EXPENSES</u> BOX**, which is your beautiful Treasure Chest.

<u>If this is too complicated for your life:</u>
1. List ALL expenses on a daily index card for a 30 day period.
2. Carry a little notebook with you. Attach a pencil or pen to the notebook for convenience.

This notebook can take the place of getting receipts. Although getting receipts is a great practice if you own a business because you can deduct a lot of things from your taxes—if you have receipts, or use the notebook when your purchases or **money spent** have no receipt (like parking meters), or use your palm pilot.

There is no right or wrong here.

If you don't get a receipt, write what you spend in your little notebook, or your palm pilot or on a napkin. How you do it isn't important; just do it.

This is about research/tracking. If you forget to save a receipt or write down an expenditure, recall as best you can that evening when you are putting your daily receipts or notebook page in your **In Daily Expense Treasure Chest**.

Be sure to include coffee, teas, LATTEs, lunch, groceries, parking meters, unattended parking garages, cookies, bagels, sundries, etc. Continue the list here…if you like.

Completion for Tool #6

After 30 days, add up all the receipts and all the other **In Daily Expenses** from your notebook, palm pilot or index cards. This will allow you to see how close you are to the original amount on your *where you spend your money* list.

How did you do?_____ (Remember most people underestimate by 25%.)

Adjust your ***where you spend your money*** list to reflect any differences you discovered between what you thought you were spending and what you actually do spend, after keeping track of your spending for 30–60 days.

This knowledge will yield you money rewards.
Your choices will become clearer.
You could master the art of handling your money flow.
You'll know how much money you will need each month.
You can make choices about what works $$wise in your life and what doesn't work.
You could get out of credit card debt.
<u>**If you think the process is silly, read on…**</u>

Tool Stories

A wonderful woman from my coaching group made this discovery: Each day she would stop at the coffee shop and purchase a $3.50 LATTE Grande. She usually only drank about half the drink. She reported that what she really wanted was a cup of coffee with a little extra milk.

After we talked, she switched to what she had wanted all along.
The outcome—The latte was $3.50 per day. The coffee was $1.08 per day. She saved $2.42 per day, $48.40 per month and $580.80 per year.

A seminar participant shared that she never paid for her groceries with cash. She put everything on her credit card. She had no idea how much she would spend during the month. She did not save the receipts, nor did she save the credit card slips. When the credit card statement arrived, if she couldn't pay it all off, she would pay whatever portion she thought was reasonable.

As we talked, the Light came on! She realized she was paying *interest* on her groceries. This was unacceptable. Astounded, she began to undo this habit. Working the muscle of "choice."

She now pays for her groceries with cash. She puts money away in her **Angel Envelopes** (a tool coming up next). She's discovered the power of choosing. (**Tool: Let's Talk Credit Cards**)

Challenge yourself to be rigorous in your money choices. It's about your abundance and prosperity. It is how you love yourself financially healthy.

CELEBRATE, NOW!

Stars _____ Here.

Tool #9
<u>Angel Envelopes:</u>

Tool #9 is a key to mastering the flow of money.

This practice keeps you on *the mark* for monthly money requirements. It is simple. It is fun. It is a way of practicing organizing your monthly money. **<u>Angel Envelopes</u>** assist you in recognizing what you need and when you'll need it.

<u>**Angel Envelopes**</u>? One day several of my colleagues and I had finished decorating our envelopes so they were fun and colorful, and we were sitting around searching for a name for our creations, which we would use for **Tool #9**. For about an hour we brainstormed all kinds of names for our creation, but to no avail. Finally, Allen's daughter, Molly, (she was four), walked into the room. She took one glance at the stickers and colored envelopes and declared, "Angel Envelopes." So they are!

Angel Envelopes is the tool of ministering to your money—abundance. It shifts the energy flow of your money to financial viability, balance and blessings.

Tool #9

Use as many envelopes as you have items on the list from <u>Where You Spend Your Money</u>—*WUSY$$$$.*

Make a few extra decorated envelopes, just in case. (We used stickers, Crayolas, drawings, watercolors, glitter, computer-generated graphics, etc.) If you don't want to do the art. Don't do it.

Energize each envelope with Loving Energy.

The idea of all the attention to these envelopes is to give you a place to awaken the loving, rich, abundant energy of your money.

MONEY TOOLBOX FOR WOMEN

When you're ready to begin simply follow these easy steps:

1. Take the WUSY$$$$ List and divide the total monthly number by the amount of times you are paid in one month.
2. On the left side, put the total amount due for the month.
3. On the right-hand side, depending on how you get paid, put the amount due each pay period.

HOW OFTEN YOU GET PAID divided INTO each EXPENSE for MONTH EQUALS $_____ on the **Angel Envelope**.

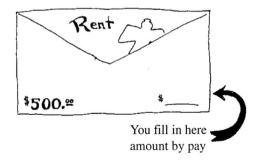

You fill in here
amount by pay

Angel Envelopes

How do you get paid?

For example: If the rent is $500.00 per month and you're paid daily, then $500 divided by 30 = $16.66 to be put into the Rent Angel Envelope each day.
Paid weekly: $500 divided by 4 = $125.00 each week into the Rent Angel Envelope.
Paid bimonthly: $500 divided by 2 = $250.00.
Paid monthly: its $500.00 into the envelope when you get paid.

Use this practice for each envelope. Yes, this means do it for each item you have on the _WUSY$$$$_ list or new items from the **In Daily Expenses**. It is time consuming… yes. You are worth the time! You only have to do it once for each envelope. Make it a game. Invite friends over to help: family, your spouse, and the kids…

Put the envelopes in the Treasure Chest in Alphabetical Order, so they are easy to find. This will keep them in an orderly and respectful manner. Money likes that energy and it will keep the flow open, easy and full of grace.

Give yourself a great celebration for getting this far. Celebrate in the way you love best. Take a moment to be grateful for all the abundances in your life.

Originally, I recommended cash only for the **<u>Angel Envelope</u>** practice. Cash is the preferred method of working with the **<u>Angel Envelopes</u>**. However, after experimenting with this method in several seminars and listening to women, I heard the fears and issues about cash in the house. Also, they expressed difficulty in getting started with cash only. So, we developed an alternative using checks: When you deposit the money from your paycheck into your checking account, write a check for each **angel envelope** made out in its particular amount.

If you have a checking account, go ahead and write the check on a weekly, bimonthly or monthly basis, depending on how you get paid.

No checking account, then its cash in the envelopes.
(When any part of a tool doesn't work for you be inventive. Do the process.)

Keep it simple for yourself. The envelopes hold the monthly money focus. They are your training wheels in this new money practice.

Use this practice until you get the rhythm of the money in your life.
You'll understand how much money you need to earn or where you will make different choices. Debt or Freedom is your choice.
This Tool gives you a key into an abundant world.

Celebrate Your New Tools and Practices. YIPPEE!
Star_____Here.

Tool #10
<u>STUFF !</u>

The tool, mini tools and tool stories combined on the next few pages, are like a *Swiss Army Knife*. Lots of Lusciously Simple information in one tool. There's no deprivation or lack – this is the place of rigorous speaking, questions, and conscious choosing.

Have Fun with this Tool. It is a resource for you to design new practices that lead to behavioral changes. (Meaning, if something's not working, change it.) With **Tool #2**: <u>**Snapshots,**</u> we looked into the past. **Tool #10**: <u>**STUFF**</u>, changes how you speak to yourself and to others. It changes your actions.

This tool changes your internal money conversations (inner voice money whispers). It will change how, when and where you spend your money. Its sole purpose is to awaken the **Choice Maker** in you. Embrace the new or different aspects of choosing.

At this very moment, with all your new abilities and knowledge about money, are you ready to learn to nurture your choices? Dream your future! You are standing at the doorway to another dimension.   OPEN IT!

Come on, this is not the time to be shy! Unlatch it. Hear the sound of the clasp letting go and then see the sun streaming through from the other side.

Now that the door is opening for you, we can proceed into the land of **money choices**. The intention is for you to realize your abundance. Through this door is your opportunity to be financially competent through the tool of **questions**.

Now is the opportunity to explore *STUFF.*

We are going to examine material wealth. The subtle differences between stuff and abundance.

Come on, explore!

Abundance may or may not include more *stuff*. There is nothing wrong with it either way. *STUFF IS JUST STUFF!* Enjoy the concept of simplicity. Enjoy the concept of spending. Do they conflict for you?

Listen to your **inner knower** (that wise question-asker that lives inside of you). Listen to what is for you and what is not: What you think you want in the moment. What you really desire on a deeper level. That place in your bones. That place that can be satisfied with nothing and everything both at the same time.

MINI - TOOLS
ELIMINATING IMPULSE SPENDING:

When it comes to Impulse Spending, DON'T DO IT. WHEN YOU GO SHOP-PING, KNOW WHAT YOU CAME TO SPEND YOUR MONEY ON AND JUST BUY THOSE THINGS. MAKE A LIST BEFORE YOU SHOP AND STICK TO IT. This is especially important in the grocery store. *My mother told me not to shop without a list.* Know what you want and spend your money on your intended purchase.

Simple Wisdom: Do not shop for food when you are hungry.
Don't shop for anything when you are feeling empty; emotionally, physically, spiritually.

Bargain Trolls:

Women, especially, have confided that sometimes they don't ask any questions of their **inner knower** before they shop. Kimberly (that's right, my daughter) is one of these individuals. I'm not picking on her, she admits shopping is an addiction. She can go out to the mall for the day, window shopping with girlfriends, with no agenda. They might be feeling depressed or lonely and have assumed shopping will nurture them, and fill the void. This can all be subconscious, not in your face. Deadly disaster.

An important concept: A bargain is a bargain only if it is something that you want and you attain it at a lesser price than you originally thought you would pay for it. A bargain is not a bargain if you received a discount and did not want or need the item prior to the "bargain trolls" showing up.

Bargain Trolls: These elusive creatures suck out your brain and tell you, "get me, get me now…take me home….," and you do. Once home, they gleefully laugh and PUT THEMSELVES AWAY IN YOUR CLOSET with the tags still on, never to be seen until you

clean out that closet or drawer years later. By that time they have multiplied several times over and you wonder how you could have several of the same (sweaters/tee shirts/toothpick holders/fill in yours): _____.
Beware of **BARGAIN TROLLS**.

Tool Story:

When a friend's Mother passed away, we cleared her closets. She really had **Shoe Bargain Trolls**. At least a hundred pairs of shoes, half never worn.
Shoe Trolls!!
I wonder if Immelda Marcos (wife of a former President of the Philippines, known for her over spending) ever asked herself, " Do I have as many shoes as I need?"
Obviously she had more than she'd ever need. More than she wanted? Obviously not. More than she could ever wear? Most assuredly.

The real question is, did she have an internal question about any of these choices?
The answer: Not from any observable behavior.

A Day Without Questions –A Shocking Concept.

I've been blessed with a curious mind and a ready questioner. But in my days of extravagance and keeping up, I lost the questions that could have saved me a lot of money. I've regained this skill. Thanks to my friend, Marilee Goldberg-Adams, Ph.D., who writes in *The Art of the Question*, "The fundamental goal is to establish an awareness of the existence of internal dialogue, the prevalence of internal dialogue, and the power of internal dialogue, so you can take advantage of this information…for the rest of your life."

When and where do we ask these self-realizing questions? Where do they lead us? *To better choices*.

Tool Story

My girlfriend, Jona, and I were shopping for a new winter warmy vest; at least that was the stated agenda. HAH! We were in this fabulously friendly sporting goods/women's wear boutique looking at the lime green vests, the bright yellow ones, and the rich embossed purple vests.

The shop had several other colors that we both ignored: red, blue, black, orange, and fuchsia. Jona tried on the yellow one and I had on this luscious purple vest. In the middle of our modeling, chatter, and indecision, the shop owner asked if we'd tried on the other colors, which we had both unconsciously ignored.

To our amazement and horror I blurted out, "No, we have most of those colors." *We BURST* into laughter. We laughed so long and hard, our stomachs hurt, while tears rolled down our faces. We couldn't breathe.

We both knew the question: What are we doing here? We have vests. "Do we want, need or desire another vest?"

Between the two of us, we have several. We wear the same size and often share clothes. We had both recognized our ***Unrecognized Abundance***!

We'd never asked ourselves any questions about the shopping day. What was the real reason we were shopping? We wanted to be with each other, playing and sharing experiences.

We had asked no relevant questions about our vision for the time we had together. What was our desire or dream for the day. From that moment forward, a new tool was instituted: *Questions First*.

If you don't normally ask yourself questions, here are a few to get you started. These questions always make me aware and help to formulate a focus for the day.

Practice: Choose one question for the day. Know that your focus can change or it can stay the same for many days. Let focused questions work for you.

Questions:

What is it I really want to do today?

What is my focus for the…morning/afternoon/day/evening/etc.?

Do I want anything? (You can substitute the words need or desire in these questions.) If so, what do I want?

What is it that I really want to get out of this?

Mentally?　　Emotionally?　　Physically?　　Spiritually?　　Financially?

Am I feeling depressed?　Will this (item) make me feel better?

Do I feel deprived?　Will this (item) create value for me?　Am I satisfied?

What is its purpose?　What is the value?

Do I have one of these already? How will I feel about it tomorrow?

Is this the way I want to spend my money $$$$, today?

How many hours did I have to work to pay for this item?

If questions are a ***new tool*** for you, be *patient* with yourself.

Tool #11
Watch Your Speaking

You will notice the words, *buy or buying,* have been eliminated from the vocabulary used in your new **money life**. When we say "Buying" it is like using a mind pacifier. What's really going on? What are we really doing? What is the event? Spending *MONEY.*

Language and the rigor/discipline of the words you use are so important. We put ourselves to sleep unmindful of our words. This is demonstrated in our actions: *Sleep Talking.* This applies internally, that little voice we hear inside, as well as what we speak externally.

Change your inside and outside speaking. Change your spending behavior.

Do I have any money to spend?

Do I want to spend money today?

How much can I spend today?

The **spending trolls,** like their cousins, **bargain trolls,** whisper, "You have a credit card."

Here is the question: DO I HAVE ANY **MONEY** TO SPEND?

Credit cards are great, don't get me wrong. However, that's not the answer to your question. These questions are clear and specific. They bring you into the present, with a view of what you already owe and a future view of the consequences.

Do you have the money? Yes! Do you want to spend it?
Do you have the money? No! Do you want to be in Debt?

Mini - Tool
Muscle Testing

The **mini-tool** is how to self muscle test. We will use muscle testing with **Tool #12: Kinesthetic Carrying Around Method or K-CAM,** the art of appreciating stuff in the moment.

Muscle testing is letting your muscular structure and your **inner knower** give you YES/NO feedback from your cellular level. It is about you knowing what is for your highest good.

There are other methods to muscle test. This is the way of doing it when you are making decisions on your own.

The 2-finger method.
This may seem silly. Relax and be silly with me for a moment.

Left hand using your thumb and first finger - form a circle, like the universal sign for OKAY. Insert Right thumb into the left hand's linked finger circle, and close the right thumb to right first finger forming two connected links.

Here's a PICTURE >>>>>

Now say to yourself or out loud, "Show me a NO." Try to pull the linked circle fingers apart. Really pull on the fingers; if they come apart (don't just let go, try keeping them linked) that's your cellular directive for "NO". Ask a question that can be answered with a yes/no answer. Example: Am I Purple? Y/N
If they stay together, that would be your symbol for NO (unless, of course, you are purple).

Now say to yourself or out loud, "Show me a YES," and try to pull the linked fingers apart. The physical response should be the **opposite** from the NO response. In this way, you will know how your body will answer questions from a cellular level. **Test it here !**

Once you have your parameters set, you're ready to gain some real wisdom from the best source there is: Yourself.

Remember, marketing companies and retailers depend on your spontaneous impulsive spending habits. That's why they put STUFF in the check-out area. Check it out for yourself next time using questions that are yes/no answers. Use K-CAM Muscle Testing: **Tool #12**. Do I need this? Want it? Have to have it? Is it for my highest good? See if it's your true self's desire or instant gratification.

Play with this! Have a good time! It sometimes takes a few tries for you to believe it works. And when it does, you'll say, "Oh yeah, I knew it would work all along!"

Tool #12
K-CAM: Kinesthetic Carrying Around Method

Tool #12: The ART of Appreciating Stuff in the Moment.
Use this method to see if you really want something or if it is a momentary whim.

You're in a store. It's filled with great stuff! For me, it's teddy bears. I have a difficult time resisting anything whimsical. For you, it could be jewelry or

_____.

I see this great bear. My internal conversation is, "I really want it!"

So, I'll pick it up and carry it around with me in the store. If it's a try-on thing, I try it on. I luxuriate in the feelings and the ability to enjoy it in the moment. In the case of the bear, I carry it around, talking with it, feeling the great furriness, cuddling it, having a great moment of possibility or what-if.

When it's time to go, I ask myself abundant, rich, nurturing questions about wanting the item, its value, and is the experience complete. (Go back and look at the questions in **STUFF**.) If the answer is YES, I spend my money and go home satisfied. If the answer is NO, I put it back, thanking the (bear—or whatever) for the time we have spent together, fully satisfied.

If I've been trying on a piece of jewelry or clothing, I ask the questions. (Check for full satisfaction.) Am I fully satisfied and full from this experience? If the answer is "YES," I thank the sales person and go.

Muscle Test. Ask your body. Check for Bargain and Spending Trolls.

Mini-Tool

You can pull the **bargain and spending trolls** towards you if you repeatedly ask the same question while you are checking out an item, over and over. They will hear the resistance to the answer and appear. Then they will whisper in your ear, "Take it home, go ahead." This is a really good time to resist their tempting plea.

What if the answer is truly a "yes?" Buy it. It's just what you've been looking for, it is beautiful, it makes you feel good—especially if you came looking for this particular thing. Spend your money here. Enjoy it. Love yourself for having found it. Be grateful.
Be grateful you have the money to spend. You do have the cash in your **Clothing Angel Envelope,** don't you?

No, there is no money in the **Angel Envelope.** Then think it out again with a different question. Ask yourself, "Will this impact my life and finances tomorrow?"

Be creative with your questions. As you do, you will learn what to ask to get the clear and best direction for you.

We all have favorite places we go when we are not being nurtured and want to fill our lives with stuff to be full. Where are some of the places or for what items could you use the **K-CAM** process? How could it be useful for you?

List them here…Now.
I find this very useful when I'm about to spend my money on potato chips. Or ring dings. Or have a third Latte Grande with (what's your favorite topping?)

_____.

What are your questions?

What is your speaking?

How will this Tool shift your spending?

More places and things spaces:

The rest of this page is intentionally left blank for your questions and answers.

Celebrate!

Star_____Here.

Mini – Tool
Refrigerator-to-Trash-Can Savings

Trash Can Savings. What we stop throwing away in our trash cans can save us a BUNDLE. Pay attention to those science experiments that grow in your refrigerator. What are you throwing away!

Recently we've become conscious of how much food was becoming outdated or overripe in the refrigerator, waiting for someone to eat it. We began to keep track, using a magnetized pad on the fridge door.

Tracking showed—yes—we were throwing away about $12.00 of food a week. Repeat buys that always got thrown away. Foods that didn't get eaten in time:

    Spoiled milk - (we started buying smaller containers)

    bananas – now black and mushy

    wilted veggies (why? forgotten)

leftovers, left over for too long.

the Doggie Bags that the dog never got. (I don't even have a dog!)

Make lists to remember what was trashed.

Why didn't it get eaten last time? Are we traveling next week?

Do we ever eat this?

If you are tracking your grocery store spending while you find what foods you're throwing away, you just might be surprised how much farther your grocery money goes with your new awareness.

Be sure to celebrate yourself for supporting yourself in paying attention. Maybe indulge in a gourmet grocery item you might not ordinarily buy. (If it's chocolate, so much the better.)

Tool #13
<u>LET'S TALK CREDIT/DEBIT CARDS</u>

Listen! Carefully.

Tool #13 is about credit and credit cards; spending and choices (this includes debit cards). It's a conversation and it has some suggestions. It is the beginning of cash in your pockets and abundance in your life.

Are you a credit card spending machine? I used to be. I taught Kimberly to be a credit card user.

Do you tend to live your life on a credit basis…rather than a cash basis? It's in our culture.

Spend now, we'll have the money later. But do we? That's part of the **Where You Spend Your $$$$** support. From there, it's a matter of what nurtures you most: Having money or not having it.

If you are going to use a credit card, be wise. Use the Tools in ***STUFF***; the skills and questions that assist you in making choices differently.

OH GODDESS, a Tool still to come discusses the new way of observing the *inside speaking* you might have about how you spend your money, and gratitude.

Tool Story
In our society it is useful to have a credit card for travel/service/renting a car, and

so on. Here's a great example of changing behavior.

The woman in this story, like so many others I have spoken with, had bottled water taste with a tap water budget. She really knew how to flash those credit cards. She was in debt up to her ears. There was just enough space left to hear her *inner knower's* screamed, *"**Cut up the credit cards!**"* It was time to learn new practices, and use those practices to pay off debt.

The approach she used was to get one credit card to use in emergencies or when credit cards are useful. This would apply to car rentals, where the rental agencies want a shipload of cash if you don't have a credit card with credit available on it. (Even there, she learned to put the car on a contract with a credit card and then pay the bill in cash when she returned the car to the rental agency.) The woman in the story discovered credit cards were a convenience and a gift.

She also used her credit card when she didn't want to carry so much cash with her.

But she now has the cash available from either her **<u>Angel Envelopes</u>** or her **<u>Cookie Jar</u>** *(which you'll learn about later)*.

The payoff here for a debt–a-holic was that when she applied her new practice of paying cash, she found herself being more aware of what she was spending.

What's more, she found that many of the kinds of things she used to buy were not really things she wanted or desired—so she was excited to have the savings and not the *stuff*. This dear lady now has loads more cash available to pursue her passions and desires.

What are credit cards to you?

What are some questions that you can make up for yourself that will be valuable to ask before you spend your money?

Write them here. Write them now.

How do I save money for what I want?
Use **Tool #14: <u>COOKIE JAR</u>**. Save the cash—before you go to buy something—so you have the money to pay the credit card debit as soon as the credit card statement arrives. Check it out for yourself…does this new tool nurture you?

Use your credit card when appropriate. Look inside yourself to make that decision. Look around in your material life to see what you already own, before you go spending your money.

Make sure you have the best interest rate you can get.

Pay it off as much as you can over the minimum each month.

Better yet, pay it all off. Or *cut up the card,* if you are a chronic user. Otherwise, you'll end up paying for that service, product, or meal over and over again.

Department store credit cards limit your choices.

"But Mom, it was the only credit card I could get," Kimberly announced, the proud owner of a high-end department store credit card, crushed that I wasn't thrilled for her. Then she began to use the card for things she had historically bought at a discount store. Kimberly explained, "I have more cash this way. I can pay it off by paying the minimum each month."

I was amazed. We talked. She was spending more on interest than she ever realized. Around 25%! Kimberly was in shock.

Simple Wisdom: *It's in the store's best interest, not yours, for you to have their credit card.*

Discoveries:

#1. Using the store card, it limited Kimberly's choices. She *had* to buy there. She did not get the best price. This high-end store cost compared to similar—or even identical—items in a discount store was 10 – 25% more.

#2. Once she'd made the purchase, the interest was 18% compounded. If she paid it off entirely each month the interest wouldn't matter. But that never happened. And, she still would have paid more for the item when she purchased it.

#3. If she paid the balance over time…she paid for the item by at least 28 - 38% over what she would have paid for it in the discount store with cash (because she paid more for it at the register, then paid again and again for it, as she paid interest on the balance remaining every month).

We didn't cut up the credit card. We used the system to establish better credit.

Kimberly is learning when she uses her major credit card to put cash towards the statement payment each time she gets paid, so she can pay off, or at least pay down, her balance. Normally she would have spent the money. Now, she puts it in her **<u>Angel Envelope</u>** and pays off her debt every month.

Mini-Tool: Getting the most from credit cards

No credit? Acquire a good credit rating. Start slow. Get a small loan at the bank but don't spend the money. Put it in a savings account and pay the loan back each month out of it, until it's all paid up. It's a start. It will cost you a little, but the rewards are worth the interest cost. You can move up from there.

Get the best interest available on major credit cards. Interest rates do vary—by a lot. Some credit cards have interest rates as low as around 9 or 10% while others are over 20%. Building her credit and qualifying for a lower rate, increased Kimberly's choices. Her first card was at a bank and had a very limited line of credit. She used it wisely and she's building her resources.

I never recommend credit cards. I use mine only so I don't have to carry a lot of cash with me. I pay them off every month. However, in the real world, credit cards and monthly credit payments are difficult to eliminate. Be Wise: Get the best rate of interest. *Make Wise Shopping Choices.* Remember the **bargain trolls** in the Tool: ***STUFF.***

Keep your options open.

Use the **<u>Where You Spend Your $$$$ Daily Tracking</u>** and **<u>In Daily Expenses</u>** to keep you focused on your intentions.

Ask Yourself Questions.

Do I need this or want this? Make the distinction.

Am I lonely, afraid, or unfulfilled and is spending a way of filling myself up?

Do I already have one or more of (item you're considering buying) _____?

Do I want/need another?

Can I live without it? Will it make a difference in the quality of my life experience?

Do I have the money (cash on hand) to spend, without causing debt in another domain of my life?

> Kimberly says she never considered the consequences of how going to dinner with her friends would affect paying her rent. Now she does.

Tool Sharpener

- •   Credit cards are the same as cash only more dangerous.
- •   Credit cards are like playing with money. You cannot see the amount you

are spending or the amounts you have spent.

- Pay off as much of the balance as you can until you are out of debt.
- Once you've done that, pay off the credit card balance each month. *You pay INTEREST on your unpaid balance DAILY. This means that what you buy today could cost you double or more, eventually, if you only pay the minimum monthly amount due.*
- Minimum balance pay-offs will keep you debt captive for *years*!
- Pay off the credit card with the highest interest rate first.
- Track your credit card spending using **In Daily Expenses.**
- Keep your credit card receipts. They're like cash if you want to return an item.
- Keep a special place for receipts of credit card purchases you want to return. These receipts are as good as money.
- Check your credit card statement. Compare what you bought with what appears on your monthly statement.
- Don't assume credit card companies do not make mistakes. They do!

- Pay on time. Late payment penalties are as much as $25.00—and often cause your interest rate to go up.
- Late payments impact your credit rating.

Celebrate!
Star_____Here.
Do what nurtures you.

Tool #14
<u>Cookie Jar</u>

*In the beauty of each step I take, I experience
myself closer to the Divine. She walks in the Light
beside me and I am grateful for the Abundances and Joys that are showered upon
me. And for all, I give thanks.* Audrey Reed.

Tool #14: Pay Yourself First. Save *today* for what you want <u>tomorrow</u>. This is about the magic of money magnets; money attracts money.

Do you pay yourself first? That concept is normally foreign to us. Women especially will tell you that they have to pay all the bills first. They make do with what is left over.

We share with others - but do we share with ourselves?

Claire, who is six, tells me, "Mommy's always too busy for me. She's too cranky for herself—she needs more naps." As adults we need to nurture ourselves abundantly.

The Point!
If we were with our best friend and had three cookies, we'd at least offer one of them to our friend. Well, offer some percentage of your paycheck to yourself, as your best friend.

Put 10% of your paycheck into your cookie jar…save it for something that you have named as a gift for yourself. The *money naming* gives focus to the line of your intention and rigor to the practice of nurturing yourself. Try it out and watch the money grow into your **money naming** (intention), which is described below.

It doesn't matter the percentage that you begin with…start today.

Count your blessings.

Be grateful for the gift, large or small.

Enjoy the flow.

Be responsible for your debt.

Be Giving (Philanthropic)

Be open to RECEIVING

Pay Yourself First.

MONEY ATTRACTS MONEY. It is not magic. It is the flow in the universe.
Money attracts money. Abundance attracts abundance.

YOUR COOKIE JAR

Find yourself a jar, a container, or cookie jar. Decorate it. Give it a name, an intention and an amount that will fill the intention.

Again, *money naming* is important. It lets the flow of abundance be energized towards your desired manifestation on the physical level.

Morsels to contemplate:
Buying stocks, one share at a time.
Seminars
Vacations
Down payment for _____.
Anniversary present
Flowers for garden
Spa Day
Manicure
Dress
Sweater
House in the country

Put 10%—or whatever is comfortable for you to do now—into your COOKIE JAR

whenever, wherever money flows to you…
Paycheck
Unexpected gifts
Tax returns—Annuities—Profits from…
A percentage of any money that comes your way.

Count your money and be grateful to have it. I send Light and Energy to the money, (just by saying, "Light and Energy to the money") and then imagine Light and Energy flowing through the money.

Let the money know how it's honored and respected.

Celebrate yourself, your loving, and loving the life you're living.
Watch the abundance, prosperity and riches grow.

(I keep a slip of paper in the cookie jar with the total amount I am moneymagneting towards. I add in each amount that is put in the jar so that I know, and the energy flow knows, when I've reached the intended amount.)

Sometimes I straighten the bills out, unfold and refold them and count the bills and the change. It is a loving action of growth, like watering and touching the leaves of flowers and plants. Sometimes when I count it, I am surprised to find more $$$$ than I thought was in the **Cookie Jar**.

Tool Story

One of my partners, Alice, and her husband were saving for a down payment on a new home. They knew about how much it would cost and began to "cookie jar" in the form of putting 10% of all money that flowed into their lives in a drawer. Her husband would put all the change from his pockets in the drawer each night, as well. Alice called the nighttime change ritual, ***Daily Money Ex Change.***

Even though they had considered the amount huge and thought it would take forever to accumulate that much, it was only about two years before they had the down payment.

Take the first step to what you want!

Mini-Tool

Money attracts Money. Part of the Money Attractor's line of energy or recognition is to keep it all in cash. This practice keeps the flow in the energy line.

DELIGHT IN YOUR SUCCESSES.
MEASURE YOUR GAINS.
TRACK THE RESULTS.
BE GRATEFUL FOR THE ABUNDANCES.
BE LOVE!
Celebrate!
Star____Here.

Tool Story

Martha's Great Aunt Harriet used to sit each morning at her kitchen table counting the household money into a large jar. So much for her husband's lunches, so much for groceries, and a few pennies into a smaller jar. Martha watched this ritual each day. She and her mother lived with her great aunt  and uncle for almost fourteen years. When she was younger, she would sit at the table while her aunt counted the money. She often wondered what the smaller jar was for, but did not have the proper question to ask her great aunt. They lived on a tiny farm, and although they were financially poor, they never seemed to want for anything. The family was rich in traditions and love. They laughed and loved the life they were living.

When Martha was seven, she asked her great aunt Harriet why she counted the money every morning. She asked her why she had three stacks of money and only two jars.

MONEY TOOLBOX FOR WOMEN

Auntie H. took both the jars off the cabinet shelf. She explained that the large jar was for the household money and the other, a small cookie jar had a large "H" and other symbols and signs painted boldly on it that were meaningful for her.

"When your great uncle Jacob and I got married, we decided, together, there would be three jars." Martha was surprised. She'd only seen two jars.

"Where's the third jar, Auntie, and what's it for?" Martha quizzed.

"The third jar I keep with my Spiritual things. It is the money for the Beloved, that we give (tithe) back for the bounty given to us," replied Harriet.

We took the other two jars and went into the master bedroom. There on her nightstand was the jar, also decorated with signs and symbols, this time of prosperity and abundance. Great Aunt Harriet explained, "The Large jar is for the House. The money that goes into that jar keeps us fed, clothed and sheltered. The jar in the bedroom is for our Spirit. It keeps the flame of grace and ease connected with the energy from which we receive to begin with. It keeps us connected to the Divine within and above."

"The other jar, so brightly painted and decorated, is for me," said Great Aunt Harriett. "It is the ten percent I pay myself. I give it a name or an intention and use it for what it is ordained to create. It is for whatever I want to manifest. I decorate it and name it and allow the mystery of the money magnet to do its work."

"Is it always for the same thing?" Martha asked.

"No, sometimes the gift is for me, sometimes a present for you, sometimes I want to buy something for Uncle Jacob and sometimes for your mother. We always pay into the jars and then celebrate the joy we bring into our lives. These cookie jars are a celebration of OUR BEING on the Planet."

Martha smiled, and asked if someday she could have her own jar. "Yes, right now. Come choose a jar and after dinner, you can decorate it. I'll help you with the colors and symbols if you like." Martha was delighted.

Today, Martha is a successful chiropractor and she continues to use this method of attracting abundance into her life. Her observation is that it has worked through the years. It has been a demonstration of how to have dominion over her fate. How to grow the abundance of life and celebrate herself with God's Divine Loving.

"I have grown to give to myself 10% of all money that flows into my hands and I share this abundance with God by tithing (giving—being philanthropic). It is my safety net, it is my loving privilege," Martha smiles. "The giving reminds me of the lessons and times I was privileged to spend with my aunt. She gave me 100% of her gentle, kind spirit; a Beloved Angel here on this earth."

Tool #15
I Still Have Checks –
I Must Have Money!

Tool #15 is about balance. Balancing your checkbook or anywhere else you have a credit/debit accounting. This includes your debit cards. It is about staying in balance and staying awake in life to live an **abundant money life**.

Tool Story

My manicurist and I were talking one day about this book and the concept of money. She really believed in the concept *I still have checks, so I have money*. What was her thinking? She hadn't balanced her checkbook in seven years, since she'd opened the checking account. She had never opened any of the bank statements to see if she was even close to agreeing with the bank's accounting. Diana just knew she had money.

Diana begins:
"Well, I know how much money I spend monthly from my account. I always deposit about $100.00 more than I know I'll spend, as a safety net. I round my checks up to the nearest dollar."

"Do you keep a running balance in your checkbook?"

"Sometimes I see if the amount I have spent that month and the amount deposited for that one month balance."

"And does it?"

"Yes, with some left over."

"How much left over?"

"Normally $50 - $100."

My mind began to calculate: 7 years X 12 months = 84 months X (let's use $75 as the average) = $6,300.00. There could be an excess of $6,300.00 sitting in a non-interest-bearing checking account. YIPPEE!!

Diana was stunned. "Do you mean six thousand three hundred dollars!?"

Diana said that all these years her strategy had been not to be **overdrawn**. That was the biggest fear. It never occurred to her that she could have SAVED that much.

I invited her to come and see me the next day with the last bank statement. I would buy the tea, she would bring her last statement. It was a real stretch for her because she was more comfortable with her habit of not knowing. Even if she found she had extra money, knowing would bring about a change in her habits, and most people don't like this kind of fundamental change, even if it's to their benefit. Eventually, Diana accepted.

Excitement in the Morning
Total$$$$

The next morning, Diana showed up with two friends to calm her nervousness. I had asked her not to open the bank statement until our meeting.

We ordered tea, laughed about the possibilities, then Diana and I agreed she would put all the extra money she discovered into a fund for her new grandson.

The suspense was killing her friends. Diana was not sure she wanted to recover this money. She was afraid.

We opened the envelope and turned back the statement. Total balance - <u>$7,897.64</u>. This new grandbaby was going to have a good start in his Trust Fund. Marvelous!

Was it a good thing that we discovered this money? Yes. Would it have been saved if she'd known it was there earlier? Good Question. I don't know the answer to that piece of history. What was revealed to her and to her friends was that they had no conscious relationship with their money. ***Now they do! And we released the fear concern by using the Tool:*** <u>**Snap Shot Methodology**</u>. Changing her inner **money pictures** that changed her perception.

Kimberly's reaction to balancing her check book: "You want me to do all this other stuff and now you want me to do *what*!? How much time do you want me to be spending on my money?" What she saw after we had begun the process, though, was that it was all done for her, to have some control over her own **money life**. With that awareness, her response was different. She adopted the point of view that the practice is about how much she could love herself financially healthy.

Tool Sharpeners

These ***tool sharpeners*** are simple and easy. There are only a few for checking accounts and other credit/debit accounts.

DO THIS FOR YOURSELF: Balance your checkbook each month.

Banks make mistakes.
Banks charge service fees.
Banks are banks…they are not GODS.
Banks are Businesses.

So you haven't balanced your checking account in __ years. Well, now is a good time to start. It really isn't that hard. Once you do it a couple times you'll find it's easy. Honest. If you don't want to go back to the beginning (that can look like a monster task), then start with this month's statement. If you've trusted the bank up until now, fine. However, from now on, let's be responsible for your money in a new and different way.

If it is just too much to think about…hire someone to do it for you, enroll a friend to assist you out of the goodness of his or her heart. Or, open a new account and start fresh. Go to the bank manager and tell him/her what you are doing. He/She will usually assist you. Take the risk.
Star _____ Here. Good Work!

A simple balancing strategy. Make a list each month of the following:
Money   Deposits   Checks   ATM
(Balance from the previous month)

At the bottom of each column there will be a total:

$—————————— $———— $———— $————

Add the Money column to the Deposit Column Total.

Subtract checks written and ATM withdrawals. Also subtract any service fee listed on the statement from the total of the money and deposit balance.

Formula:
Money Starting In Account (from statement)+ Deposits = Total Money
Less (subtract)
Checks + ATM + Service Fees
Equals =
Money Balanced $ _____

This simple practice will give you your balance. If there is a difference between your number and the bank's balance, check to see if all the checks you have written have been cashed or that all the ATM deposits or withdrawals have been listed. (Yes, save the ATM slips and debit card slips; make note of them in your checkbook so you have a record of the withdrawal.)

Check to see if all the deposits have been listed. This should bring your statement up to date.

Too complex: Use a big yellow sheet of paper to do the easy math. There is a form on the back of most bank statements, but it is probably too small to do the calculations on. Be sure to have a calculator and pencils.

Or do it on your computer. (There is a fantastically easy software called Quicken that is an easy-to-use, extraordinarily automated computer program. It makes entering your checks each month a breeze and makes balancing your checkbook with the statement almost fun.)

Any way you choose, do this practice every month. It will keep you present and aligned with the energy of money. It will help you understand the relationship of the numbers to the actual money.

Need more help? Go to the bank and again request assistance or get a friend, family member, business associate, bookkeeper, etc., to assist you the first few times.

Tool Sharpener Reminder

Check your credit card statement against your credit card receipts. Keep your ATM and Debit Card slips to check against your bank statements.

At the very least, throw the receipts into a drawer with the date clearly marked on the slip with a thick magic marker. Keep the slips until the credit card statement comes and you've checked the slips against your statement.

Make sure the amounts are the same. Make sure you have not been double charged. Make sure you haven't been charged for something you didn't order or *didn't want to spend your money on.*

DO IT for yourself…
DO IT to nurture your financial future…
DO IT to keep the money abundantly flowing in your life…
DO IT FOR YOUR SPIRIT…

Star____Here!
CELEBRATE!

Tool #16
Circle of Loving

Tool #16 is about **Relationship Money Talk**. It is about you and your family and how you talk about money together.

Tool Story

I could hear the couple arguing in the waiting room. I listened to their anger and fear. It was about money. It was about responsibility. It was about communication about money. It was about being willing to listen to each other's concerns.

Tool #16 is about **relationship money talk**, both speaking and listening. Money is an area where relationships get stuck. *Money talk* impacts most other areas of living; as an individual, as a parent, as a couple, as a family, as a village and as a global community.

When you, as an individual and in a family unit, are successful about appreciating the other people in your life, there will be success in all you focus on and all you dream.

Do any of these phrases sound familiar?

I've done a good job. What makes you think you can do it better?
If there were more money or more _____. . .if we had spent less…then things would balance out.
It's not the math…it's the money.
I'm afraid.
You don't appreciate what I do.
All you do is accuse and disrespect the job I'm doing.

What is your hot button conversation around money?

I have asked men and women this very question for the past three years, while doing research for this book. Whose job is it to be responsible? What we've heard can be summed up into two responses:
It's hers. She's the one who. . . .
It's his. He's the one who. . . .

The finger of blame and shame points to the darker side of the flow of money. Is there ever enough? How, as a couple, can you talk about money in a way that nurtures the relationship?
The last question: Whose responsibility is $$$$?
Answer: It is everyone's!

Tool #16
WELCOME TO THE CIRCLE OF LOVING

Ellen, a **Money ToolBox** Seminar participant stated, "My husband and I used to blame everything on one another. A deadly discussion. We did it every month. Every month the bills tore at the heart of our loving. We hurt each other with our words."

When it comes to money, many people do that. So we looked for something that could help change it. We found the solution in a most interesting place.

Kimberly and I have been studying Native Peoples' Rituals for years. One of the practices we learned about is the ***talking stick.*** It is used for all types of heartfelt, open communications and is a practice that has been used for centuries by Native Peoples in Council Meetings. I thought the ***Talking Stick Ceremony*** would be useful for couples in their money talks.

MONEY TOOLBOX FOR WOMEN

Mini-Tool

The person with the stick talks, uninterrupted.
The person or people without the stick listen, without interrupting.
When the speaker is complete, there is a signal; I'm complete or thank you or
A HO! (This is a part of the tradition.) The stick is then passed to the next person
on their left…so it moves clockwise.

When the next person receives the talking stick, it is their turn to speak.

The Preparation:
Draw an imaginary circle on the floor. Make the circle large enough to sit in comfortably. Fill the circle with pillows and fuzzy blankets; things that make you comfortable. Use chairs if you like.
Light some candles in a safe place.
Select an object that will represent a _**talking stick.**_

Ideas - for the object the speaker will hold, use a crystal, a heart pillow, a favorite pendant, a stick.

The Process: (read the instructions first)
Step inside the **<u>Circle Of Loving</u>.**
Take the stick or representation with you.
Sit down, get comfortable.
The person who has the stick speaks.

Make sure the stick gets passed so both people get a chance to speak.
Agree to an amount of time each person will speak before passing the talking stick. You can do this by passing the stick every 5 minutes or so. When you first start this practice, USE A TIMER. Keep your agreement with each other. It's part of the process.

Determine how long the circle will remain set, before you begin.
Not less than 30 minutes. No longer than an hour.
No one leaves the circle during the talking.
Breather Moments: Every 10 minutes or so, take a breather; 2 or 3 deep breaths.

Addition for our practice:
The speaker may want to stop, every once in a while and ask if anything requires clarifying, or they may pause just to stay connected to the listener. They would stop and ask, "Are you understanding me?"
This is for Clarification ONLY. It is not a time for the listener to take over the talking stick. The only acceptable responses are:
Yes, What I heard you say was _____.
No, I did not understand _____.

This is an element to use in your **<u>Circle Of Loving.</u>**

Guidelines and Boundaries:
Speak gently to one another. No accusations or name calling.
Look at your responsibility in the action. No Blaming.
Be present and/or future oriented. No Character Assassination for past actions.
Stay present and in the circle. Do not abandon the circle, your partner or the process.
Be respectful and loving.
Put the guidelines on a card or piece of paper, as a reminder.

This practice may be uncomfortable the first few times. Practice makes it easier. It is a tool. It takes time and practice to build the muscle of trust.

The Talking Stick is a resource to help you establish clear lines of communication. You may find that, after a while, you have naturally moved into a more loving and respectful pattern of speaking to each other and sharing. Whether you do or not, the **Circle Of Loving** is a powerful practice to use regularly.

Tool Stories

Successful **Money Talk** Ideas using the **<u>Circle Of Loving</u>**:

Every month, when it is time to pay the bills, Ed and Barbara clear away a special place on the floor in the family room. Each gathers the bills, financial data, bank statements, etc., from their respective offices or wherever. Ed brings his laptop computer and a little printer; some prior preparation seems to pay off. Barbara prefers paper, pencils, a note pad, the printed bank statement, checkbook, etc. Additional "TECHNO STUFF" stresses her out after working all day. (It doesn't matter what combination works for you…it's the process that's working.)

They bring candles, a bottle of their favorite drink (alcohol is not recommended during this although, some people like a bottle of wine), a tablecloth and napkins, great wineglasses, and a bottle of water. Ed prepares snacks, while Barbara takes a shower and relaxes for 15 minutes or so. She wears her flannel pajamas with an animal crackers design; he loves his sweats. Then they set everything on the family room floor. It's like a picnic.

This was the way they studied together in graduate school. It seemed nostalgic at first, now it is **Romantic Money Manifesting**. It's comfortable.

They light the candles, set *the circle of loving* around themselves, the bills and the picnic. This is the circle in which all things are said from a loving heart space, without harm.

Ed and Barbara say they keep the ground rules on a 3X5 card in the circle. They pass a pencil—decorated with $$$$, to represent their money—as the **talking stick**.

Barbara and Ed kiss, hug and go to work.

The first time wasn't easy. Ed didn't like sharing some of his power and information. He'd always kept all the financial information—investments, savings, mutual funds, etc. Barbara didn't like learning how controlling she was, either. She'd kept the household checking account. They worked it and worked it until it worked. There was nothing secret. Everything was held in a sacred, respectful loving way.

Another couple, Ben and Ellen report they are more satisfied and respectful of one another since they've started their **Money Circle Of Loving**. They do it at the kitchen table and have a special drawer where they keep pencils, pens, calculator, stamps, payment books, all the bills in a small file, etc., etc., etc. (They never have to go hunting for anything to do this practice; it's all in the drawer.)

Ben likes the paper flow. Ellen has her computer in a small sub-office in the kitchen. When they are ready to enter things into the computer, they expand the circle to the computer while entering the information. They snack on coffee and all natural peanut butter cookies. And yes, the candles are important.

Candles transmute and burn away negative energy.

Ellen says the best part of the circle is, once she got used to the honest, open sharing and communication, she felt closer to Ben. She's more attracted to him and they're honoring each other's opinions as partners in life. They are a Celebration of the Wealth of Their Life TOGETHER.

You could include your children in parts of the process. Very wise. This way they'll get a great experience of money, family, caring, sharing and communication.

I cannot say that this process will work the first, second or even the third time you use it. Eventually, the individuals who have been committed to the practice will find loving, open, honest and trusting common ground.

Tool Question

WHY DO WE NEED TO COMMUNICATE WITH OUR PARTNERS ABOUT MONEY?

For Husbands or Wives who don't want to share the balance sheets with each other, it is important to hear what is being said about this in the world. Statistics show women, especially, in the age range, of 60 and over, have had little financial experience with money until after they lose their spouse. (This could be the husband's situation just as easily.)

After the financial handler dies, they are lost. Left to struggle through, and learn by trial and error, or at the mercy of another. Now, in our sophisticated society, how can this be true? Several financial mangers, I have spoken with, especially in *high widow/widower* areas, say this concern is *very real.*

Wouldn't it be more effective to nurture the one you love into a *knower?* To communicate with the one you love? It can be challenging. You would have to ask questions and move into a place of trust and love. The results of **money talk** will nurture the relationship around money and each other.

It can be a difficult talk, especially for men or women who have controlled the money throughout a relationship. My former husband and I didn't even share a credit card or checking account. We never really compared financial information until the divorce.

I certainly had never been taught how to ask financial questions in a relationship from a loving heart space. I realized we were out of the **Circle Of Loving and trusting** when he consulted a financial manager and I was not invited to the meeting. I did not even think about asking to be a partner in the conversation.

We didn't handle our money fears before we got married. Money fears became our nightmare later in the relationship. Mentally we felt unable to address the subject of money as adults. It was clear he was uncomfortable with the discussion. The fear compounded itself through time. The distrust and projections of past experiences (not even ours together) were projected onto the marriage. It separated us from our loving.

Money Lesson

When I examine this situation from a place of what I would call "sacred witness," (a place of neutral observing, free of judgements) I can see how fragile and frightened I was at the time. It was an opportunity to grow and learn new practices.

Money Blessing

Things do change. Growth and expansion is good for the Soul.

Give it a try…take the time…nurture yourself, your spouse, lover, etc., and the family.

Celebrate your successes.
Star ____Here!

Tool #17
__GRATITUDE__

Oh Goddess. . .won't you. . .

Tool #17 is about gratitude. It relates several **_Tool Stories._** It will open you up to observe your day to day life with new eyes.

It is about the flow of money. It is about the energy of abundance. It is a metaphoric story This **Tool** is written in a different form from the other *tools.* *Think of it as a power tool.*

Here it is:

Write what you are grateful for from each day every night!

Tool Story:

And so there was Janis
One day most fervently
Petitioning the Goddess.
"Oh Divine,
Oh Beloved
Oh (add your preferred deity here): _____

"Please, Please,
Won't you buy me, send me, give me, deed me…
A new car."
And from the Heavens, the Goddess questioned,
"And what did you do with the car I gave you?"

"Oh, Goddess, Divine, Beloved, _____,
It got old and worn out.
The body was dented and dirty.
The inside was a mess from papers and dirt and fast food.
And the engine was sick from misuse.
Then one day it ran out of gas…"
"I see," said the Goddess, Divine Mother…

The very next day, there's Janis praying,
"Oh, Goddess, Divine Mother, Lord, _____;
Please, Please send to me a new relationship, a new husband to love me and take care of me."

"What happened to TED? Ted was a good man, with great spirit and he loved you very much?"

"Oh, Goddess…
I sent him away.
He wasn't for me—He this-ed and he that-ed and I yelled at him a lot.
I made his actions wrong.
Withdrew my love and he left me."
"I see," said the Goddess, Divine Mother _____.

And the next day there was Janis, again!
"Oh Goddess, Please, Please,
Send some money to me."
I need money to pay my bills and buy things. Please, Please, help me.
The Goddess, Divine Mother asked, "What did you do with the abundance, the prosperity, the money that has flowed to you always?"

"Why Mother, I spent it. I used it. I discarded it."

"ALL of it? You spent all of it? You saved nothing? Gave nothing? Offered nothing? You spent it all?"

"Why, yes, of course. What's wrong?"

The Goddess, Divine Mother paused, "You have a negative thought form configuration, that could prove an interesting choice."

"What does that mean?"

"Let me say it, again. Is nothing I give you sacred? Nothing?
Is nothing I give you worth caring for—worth loving, honoring and respecting?

Love yourself.
Respect others.
Love others.

Respect life.
Respect the gifts.
All that is on this planet is a gift.
Respect ALL."

The Goddess, Divine Mother flared and fire rose from her once serene being. Her gentle mouth expanded and she spoke loudly and clearly to be heard in the heart. She spoke to remind Janis to keep heart and mind open to abundant thinking.

She reached out to Janis and said, "Now is a moment of choosing with grace, honoring, loving, respect, caring, sharing, happiness or the hard way…NOTHING but wondering, searching and struggle.
Know this: abundance may not always show up the way you want it. Be grateful for what manifests. Honor all the abundances.
Otherwise, you struggle."

The Goddess vanished in a puff of smoke. All that was left was a weedy old garden with one beautiful orchid and a note…(never leave without a note).

Simple Wisdom:
Tend to me lovingly, and I will reveal all
And unfold my loving that is yours.
It will enfold you in Light and Loving.
<u>The Goddess.</u> ♪

Tool Story

Let the money flow – abundantly.
Open your heart!
Hesitation = Fear / Trust = Love

Flow into gratitude = into abundance = prosperity. It is about how gratitude affects the flow of your money and abundance.

Emilee tells her story of gratitude and expansive behavior around **money and relationships.** She was very hesitant about sharing her childhood stories, since she has "risen above those circumstances."

Emilee begins.
I was sitting on the just swept steps of my friend Jesse's house. I was fifteen. Tears were rolling down my face. Jesse's mother came to the screen door, with a glass of fresh lemonade and her most motherly voice. There were tones of laughter, just under the sincerity and concern.

"Oh girl, what is wrong? Here you are on this glorious day, getting tears on my just swept porch. Oh, Lordy, Lordy!" She shook her finger and started to laugh. It was one of those, 'I love you honey' laughs, filled with caring and the knowledge that teenage pain was normally short lived.

Mrs. Beverly Whitestone, Jesse's mother, always balanced me. I wiped away the tears. "You children, you're so fortunate. Now what is all this crying?" She petted my head and cooed a calming sound into my ear.

"You have everything," Mrs. W. whispered. "Yet, I hear you want for more. I hear you being ungrateful when you get something that is not just the way you wanted it. Respect all the gifts." She stopped and I looked around the yard with new eyes sung into being from her love.

Jesse's Mother's house was like a jewel in this neighborhood. Her determination and imagination had created a new pride from the focus of powerful loving, sheer will and action. Just around the corner, were unpainted, impoverished houses and a community that had been blind to this vision until Mrs. W and her family began to work on the house. It was as if those without the vision might have lived in the circumstances forever, if not for her model and intention.

Because of Mrs. W., home and the community are now always clean and safe. The well-planted gardens bloom year round. The blooms give off a scent of heaven, when you turn the corner into her neighborhood. The flowers are gigantic and fragrant. Mrs. W's vegetables, exquisite. They resonate with health and nutrients. The vibrant richness of her garden is sensual, intoxicating.

It was here that I learned to appreciate great wealth and abundance from the joys of life. This house had been Beverly's dream. It did not appear to match her vision when she had first discovered it. The house and property were a wreck: run down—depleted—unappreciated—overgrown—dilapidated and what else…left for greener places by others.

Mrs. Beverly Whitestone and her family had loved this little house back to health. They had painted it, nurtured it, planted roses and lavender to heal the wounds of the past, put in a garden of vegetables, hung a swing on the front porch, mowed the lawn and trimmed the trees. They had washed this house with loving, inside and outside. All these years, they had kept it just that way, each and every day. It was satisfying!

I was shaken by Mrs. W's gentle question:
"Now, tell me what this crying is, you poor child." Her voice creeping into the corners of my mind, bringing me present. "Your boyfriend broke up with you? Yes?" I was stunned—it was private. This girl/boy dance. Beverly said, "I watch you. I watch life flow into your hands and I watch as you criticize it out of your hands. You undervalue the gift and want it different."

Mrs. W. continued, "Let me tell you what Momma told me about gifts from God, this includes everything—relationships, money, friends—everything. My Momma would say, 'Know where your $$$$ is.
"'Know how much you have.

"'Know what you have to pay.

"'Choose what you want to buy.

"'Watch how much you throw away.

"'Always put some away for another day.'"

"Why, we're still finding money she put away. Not because she didn't know where it was. It was because she had so much money."

"What does this have to do with anything? Come, sit here on the swing and let me tell you some more of what my momma would say. She'd say, 'Money is like a good man - you take really good care of him; respect him, honor his SELF, his energy and celebrate life with him.

"'Laugh, dance, sing, work together, do husband and wife things together, hold hands, hug, kiss and be physical. Give him his time. He'll stay forever. You'll share the **Circle of Loving**. You'll grow rich together.

"'You treat him poorly, yell, holler, sleep on the other side of the bed, tell him he's no good, doesn't meet your standards, he'll find someone else to appreciate him.

"'Same for Men and Women - Same with $$$$ - Same with Abundance - Same with Prosperity - Same with Riches - Same with Friends - Same with Community - Same with Mother Earth. If we spend, we deplete, we live in the land of lacking...We speak into that circle of lack, girl!'"

So What!

"So when you cry those blues of **Oh Goddess**, please bring me this, please bring me that. The Lord or whoever you cry to already gave it to you once. I bet you. And I bet you spent it, gave it away, tarnished it, said it wasn't just what you wanted and you threw it away. Now, enough!" She paused and gave me a measuring look. "You better?"

I wiped my eyes and nodded. She smiled, hugged me and we both laughed. Yes, I was better.

Beverly Whitestone cut an iris from her garden and placed it behind my ear. "All the riches, all the wealth is here, now."

I took those few valuable words away that day. I, Emilee, Doubter of the World, took some of Mrs. Beverly Whitestone's gratitude and joy for life.

Later in life, I began to see the wisdom spoken by this "Wise Woman" that day on the porch, swinging on her swing, in the middle of July. She is the gift in my life.

Her Wisdom, "Gratitude, for all is the energy of abundance." Recognition of all the abundance that already exists is the pathway to creating what we want in the material world. Money is a companion to this energy. Be mindful of what is present in your life. Be respectful; honor it, care for it, appreciate the gifts that come present. Celebrate the riches and the lushness of life. Be Grateful.

 Gratitude opens up the abundance vortex, so that the energy can recognize more abundance and be attracted to like energy. Things happen. Magical things happen in this space.
HEALTH
WEALTH
HAPPINESS
ABUNDANCE
PROPSPERITY
LOVING
CARING
SHARING
JOY   RICHES   WEALTH AND TOUCHING

Can you hear it? Can you see it? Can you feel the differences?
Silence in the moment. Come present to the sound of the riches of life.

Questions to open up the energy and let the flow begin:

What are the gifts you are for yourself and others?

Where are you abundant in your life?

How are you abundant?

Who are you grateful for in your life? (I recommend a grateful segment in your journaling, each night. Writing gratitude keeps us aware of the blessings and how they flow in our lives. More on this later.)

Remember to assign an intention to your **Cookie Jar**.

Tool #18
<u>Receiving and Giving</u>

Tool #18 is simple and profound. It is about being open to receive and ready to give. That's all there is to say except for some words of advice from old friends and a Tool Story.

Tool Story:

Vera, an old and dear client of mine, once said something so astounding that I had it framed and it sits on my bookshelf: "Why would anyone want the dregs of your energy and loving?"

What did Vera mean by her statement?

Well, her explanation is that giving to people when the goblet of your life is half empty or half full, there still might be the sweetness of your loving whole energy there to resonate to them. If you give and give until the goblet is empty, then they get the residue, the dregs of your energy…and dregs are usually caustic and bitter.

Her suggestion to me and to all of us is to "Fill yourself up." Take care of yourself, first. Then care for others. If you are not full, decline until you are. If you are not topped off…decline until you are. Give from the sweet drops that overflow the cup of life. Give the sweetness of your energy and your loving. Give from the heart space of generosity and caring. Give back and you shall receive again. Be willing to partake of the flow.

The flow of the energy of abundance, wealth, prosperity and riches starts from within and spirals outward.

My wonderful wise friend and sister, Norma Deull, an abundantly balanced woman, says, "You can't receive with closed hands…open your hands and your heart." She gives back, philanthropically, personally, and from her company in so many generous ways. Her life is filled with loving light. I thank her for the lessons. I am grateful for her generosity of love.

Simple Wisdom:

Take care of yourself, so you can care for others.
Give of the Overflow.
Love yourself Abundant.
Let the energy of the Loving Flow.

Be opened to receive.
Plant a Seed by stating clearly what you want to manifest from your heart.
State Your Intentions Clearly.
Be rigorous with the languaging of your desire.

MONEY TOOLBOX FOR WOMEN

Stay Focused/Balanced

Give back into the Universe (Eventually - use the measure of 10% for your giving.)

Be Grateful.

Service is a Generous Giving and Receiving.

The Blessing will manifest unto you, as you walk the path of receiving and giving naturally.

Use the tools. Practice!

You and Your Money will prosper in this Universe.

PHILANTHROPY
(Giving)

Give of yourself
(service), your
money, your
abundance.
Live life large.

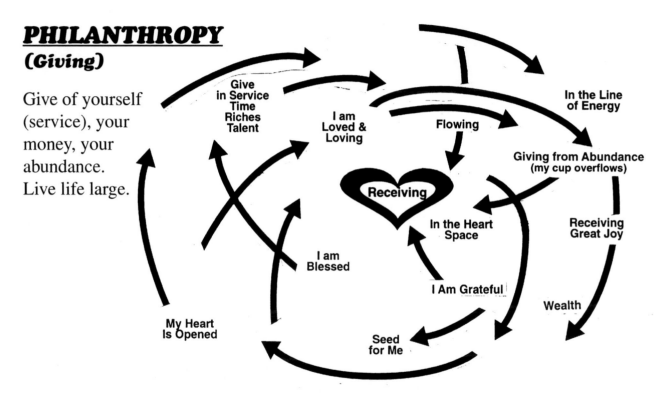

Give
in Service
Time
Riches
Talent

I am
Loved &
Loving

Flowing

In the Line
of Energy

Giving from Abundance
(my cup overflows)

Receiving

In the Heart
Space

Receiving
Great Joy

I am
Blessed

I Am Grateful

Wealth

My Heart
Is Opened

Seed
for Me

Tool #19
Nurture Yourself
Nurture Your Money
Nurture Your World

"There's only one key. There's really only one law—and that is the law of loving."

John-Roger, _Loving Each Day_

Tool Story
Rebecca's Grandmother's Sweater

A year or so ago, my neighbor Rebecca's mother passed away. Becky had been really missing her and had taken to walking around her mom's house in a quiet introspective way. One day, she called me and said she was beginning the process of sorting through years of her mom's things and could I come and be with her while she began the process. I accepted, only when she agreed we would take a picnic and a bottle of champagne to celebrate new beginnings. Becky reluctantly agreed. I picked her up and we drove about an hour to her mom's house.

On this drive, Becky spoke about the family and the house. It had always been the family house. Her Grandmother and Grandfather had built this house in 1897. It is a large white-framed house, blue trimmed, with a wonderfully overgrown garden and secret places.

We drove up the long driveway; unpruned lilac trees fragranced our arrival. The once magnificent home was now in a state of semi-disrepair. A good cleaning and some paint would give this place a new lease on life. (That's another story.)

Rebecca and I parked the Jeep and unlocked the back door. Then we stepped through the looking glass of time into her family's loving. We left the door open; a small breeze blew through and shook loose the mildew of time that was locked away in these rooms. We opened more windows, retrieved flat, unconstructed, boxes and tape from the vehicle, and spent time in the kitchen

There were stacks of old newspapers and neatly folded paper bags from the beginning of time stored on the back porch. There was a stove that had replaced a wood burning stove in the late 40's, whose cooking chores had been greasy and burdensome. It was (how do I say this?) overused and under-cleaned? YUCKY!!

When it was time to stop for lunch I rescued the champagne from the frigidaire. We decided to go up on the roof to picnic. It was flat in one area, a spot Becky had loved all her life.

We climbed the stairs and ascended into one of those fabulous old attics, loaded with treasure. And so it was. We stopped short of eating to open the one box carefully marked "MOTHER." The box was old, ragged on the corners, spidery on top. It was folded into itself, not taped. Inside were a few pieces of tissue paper and some hand-embroidered linen.

Becky was delighted. We lovingly examined the contents to discover it was her mother's mother's monogram on the linens. We'd hit pay dirt! YIPPEE! Memories of her Grandmother flooded into her; I could see them reflected on her face. We unwrapped several stained pieces and sighed with the disappointment that they had not been well cared for or honored.

At the very bottom of the box was an old satin lingerie bag, stained first from wear and then years of sitting. Becky pulled it carelessly out of the box. From the opened flap slid a soft, blue, intricately hand beaded cashmere sweater. Becky gasped and snatched it out of thin air as it hurdled towards the dusty wooden flooring. "Oh my God! This is the sweater my Grandmother wore in a picture that is on the mantel downstairs. Oh my God!" We reverently examined this masterpiece of workmanship that had survived all these years in an old satin bag in a box. It had been cared for and nurtured, kept safe and restored time and time again with tiny hand sewn stitches.

The initials MER, Mary Elizabeth Reilly, were carefully printed on the inside tag and each bead in the flower chain had been reinforced. It was deliciously soft and Becky smiled as though she had discovered gold—a treasure from the past, well cherished then, and well cherished today.

Every once in a while, Becky wears the sweater in celebration of her past. But that day, as we sipped champagne and tenderly touched each tiny bead and thread, we touched a deeper place of nurturing. We saw what tender reinforcement and appreciation could do— for a sweater, for our lives.

Questions to reinforce your nurturing:

How do you nurture yourself?

How is your family nurtured by you nurturing yourself?

When is enough, enough?

How do you reinforce your money flow?

Last word

Take a mini vacation. Each day close your eyes and take yourself away to a place that nurtures your vision, your spirit, your soul, yourself, your loving.

All will nurture your money and abundance.

Writing Space:

More Writing Space:

Open your arms
Sense the presence of the Beloved

Take a deep breath
Open yourself up to the Loving

Gently allow yourself to be Breathed
Into Paradise

Step forward into the Light
Welcome Home

Audrey Reed, Doctor of Spiritual Science

AUTHOR'S THANKS:

I am blessed by the loving I have discovered in this process, and the teachers I have referred to in John-Roger and John Morton. I am devoted to my mentor and sisters in Spiritual Work, Jyoti, Ewa and the Kayumari Community. The angels and guides, mentors and teachers who walk on this planet; my daughter, Kimberly, my mother and father Lenora Fenning and George Gross, my brother, George Gross and his wonderful wife Andrea. Those individuals who came to teach me greater lessons than I could have ever imagined, my friend for life Matthew Molitch; Howard Henis, my financial guide, my teacher Fernando Flores who taught me rigor and the power of observation, and Leslie Cameron Bandler-LeBeau, who taught me to look with a pure heart and clear mind.

I am grateful to Méschelle Kesteloot for her assistance, friendship, writing and editing. Thanks to Walter Kesteloot for the wonderful illustrations, to Lorraine Pickett for her support and steadfast assistance. My eternal thanks to Hal Zina

Bennett for taking on a first-time author and for his mentorship. Thank you to Ellen Reid, Smarketing; Laren Bright, a great wordsmith for saving my sanity; Penelope Bright and Sheila Joan Harvey for painstakingly proofing this work; Ernie and Patty Weckbaugh, Casa Graphics, cover and interior design, additional drawings and for their patience.

And to my husband, lover and spiritual partner, Stuart Green for his encouragement, his gracious loving, and devotion to my spiritual process.

I am grateful to the friends who have walked this path with me, understood my quest and stood by the warrior's side as I have journeyed there and back. Renee Singer-Goldberg, Joan Geller Solomon, Zachary Solomon, Steve Goldberg, Marilee Goldberg-Adams, Ph.D., Gaila Corrie, Marianne Sladzinski, Jona Kremp, Karen Zurlinden, Susan Stuart, Linda Noble-Topf, Michael Topf and all the many more I have not mentioned here who held the container of loving for me to begin and finish this work. They live in my heart always.

When Money Matters. . .

. . .Audrey Reed, D.S.S., The Money Doctor, can help. She has a wealth of practical, personal experience building wealth, prosperity and abundance. She has thoroughly researched how people—especially women—can gain mastery over money and their personal finances.

She is a fascinating, high-energy speaker who cuts to the chase about money issues. She is a wizard at one-on-one coaching to identify non-productive beliefs and habits. . .replacing them with new behaviors. Her integration style is light, warm- hearted and enjoyably practical.

Contact: Audrey Reed, Doctor of Spiritual Science, for speaking, seminars, workshops and personal/business coaching.
For more information visit www.draudreyreed.com or
www.moneytoolboxforwomen.com

Audry Reed, D.S.S.
Works In Progress
2118 Wilshire Blvd., Suite 771
Santa Monica, CA 90403
310/394-7687
fax: 310/394-7047
Toll free: 888/853-6564

www.moneytoolboxforwomen.com
info@moneytoolboxforwomen.com

<u>BOOK ORDERING INFORMATION</u>:   (Order Forms on Next Pages)

Order Toll Free: 888-853-6564 or (CA) 310-394-7687 (secure message machine).
  Give mailing/shipping address, telephone number, MC/Visa/AMX, name and card number plus expiration date.

Secure Fax Orders: 310-394-7047. Fill out form on next page and Fax.

On-line Orders: www.moneytoolboxforwomen.com

Email Orders: orders@moneytoolboxforwomen.com

Visit Audrey Reed
and learn more about
MONEY TOOLBOX FOR WOMEN
"Simple Solutions for Mastering Your Money"
at
www.moneytoolboxforwomen.com

Order Form

MONEY TOOLBOX FOR WOMEN *"Simple Solutions for Mastering Your Money"*

Please send me the following:

Quantity	Item	Price	
_____	*Money ToolBox for Women*/Trade Paperback	$16.00ea.	
		Subtotal	_____
		Shipping ($5 per book within USA)	_____
		CA residents add 8.25% Sale Tax	_____

Customer Information (please print)   TOTAL   _____

Name:_____

Mailing Address:_____

City:_____State:_____Zip:_____

Home Telephone:_____Fax:_____ Email:_____

Method of Payment: Check   MasterCard   Visa   Amx

Card number:_____Exp. date_____

Credit Card billing address if different from one above_____

Customer's Signature:_____Date:_____

The undersigned purchaser certifies that he has read and understands all of the terms and conditions on this invoice. All the terms and conditions are available upon request and are part of this sales order, which shall constitute a contract between parties and there are no expressed or implied warranties, modifications, or performance guarantees other than those expressly stated herein.

www.moneytoolboxforwomen.com
888-853-6564

Order Form

MONEY TOOLBOX FOR WOMEN *"Simple Solutions for Mastering Your Money"*

Please send me the following:

Quantity	Item	Price
_____	*Money ToolBox for Women*/Trade Paperback	$16.00ea.

Subtotal _____

Shipping ($5 per book within USA) _____

CA residents add 8.25% Sale Tax _____

Customer Information (please print)

TOTAL _____

Name:_____

Mailing Address:_____

City:_____State:_____Zip:_____

Home Telephone:_____Fax:_____ Email:_____

Method of Payment: Check   MasterCard   Visa   Amx

Card number:_____Exp. date_____

Credit Card billing address if different from one above_____

Customer's Signature:_____Date:_____

The undersigned purchaser certifies that he has read and understands all of the terms and conditions on this invoice. All the terms and conditions are available upon request and are part of this sales order, which shall constitute a contract between parties and there are no expressed or implied warranties, modifications, or performance guarantees other than those expressly stated herein.

www.moneytoolboxforwomen.com

888-853-6564